Reforming the African Public Sector

Author

Joseph R.A. Ayee is Professor of Political Science and Dean, Faculty of Social Studies, University of Ghana, Legon since April 2002. He obtained the BA and MPA degrees from the University of Ghana and the PhD from the Hebrew University of Jerusalem. He was appointed a lecturer at the University of Ghana in 1984, promoted Senior Lecturer in 1990, Associate Professor 1995 and Professor 1997. He was Head, Department of Political Science, University of Ghana, Legon from October 1995 to September 2000. He served as the Chair in Leadership Studies at the UNESCO/United Nations University Leadership Academy (UNULA) in 2001. He also lectured at the College of Administration, Polytechnic of Sokoto State, Nigeria and the Department of Political and Administrative Studies, University of Swaziland. He was Visiting Commonwealth Research Fellow, Department of Politics, University of Glasgow, Scotland from October 1993 to July 1994. He won the University of Ghana 2006 Best Teacher Award in the Humanities. He is a Fellow of the Ghana Academy of Arts and Sciences and the Ghana Institute of Management. Professor Ayee is the author of four books, editor of three and co-editor of one. In addition to these, he has over 120 publications as articles, chapters in books and book reviews.

Reforming the African Public Sector

Retrospect and Prospects

Joseph R.A. Ayee

Green Book

© Council for the Development of Social Science Research in Africa, 2008
Avenue Cheikh Anta Diop Angle Canal IV,
BP 3304 Dakar, 18524 Senegal
www.codesria.org

Layout: by Hadijatou Sy
Printed by Imprimerie Graphiplus, Dakar, Sénégal

CODESRIA Green Book
ISBN: 2-86978-214-4
ISBN 13: 978286972143

The Council for the Development of Social Science Research in Africa (CODESRIA) is an independent organisation whose principal objectives are facilitating research, promoting research-based publishing and creating multiple forums geared towards the exchange of views and information among African researchers. It challenges the fragmentation of research through the creation of thematic research networks that cut across linguistic and regional boundaries.

CODESRIA publishes a quarterly journal, Africa Development, the longest standing Africa-based social science journal; *Afrika Zamani,* a journal of history; the *African Sociological Review; African Journal of International Affairs* (AJIA); *Africa Review of Books; and the Journal of Higher Education in Africa.* It copublishes the *Africa Media Review* and *Identity, Culture and Politics: An Afro-Asian Dialogue.* Research results and other activities of the institution are disseminated through 'Working Papers', 'Monograph Series', 'CODESRIA Book Series', and the *CODESRIA Bulletin.*

CODESRIA would like to express its gratitude to the Swedish International Development Cooperation Agency (SIDA/SAREC), the International Development Research Centre (IDRC), Ford Foundation, MacArthur Foundation, Carnegie Corporation, NORAD, the Danish Agency for International Development (DANIDA), the French Ministry of Cooperation, the United Nations Development Programme (UNDP), the Netherlands Ministry of Foreign Affairs, Rockefeller Foundation, FINIDA, CIDA, IIEP/ADEA, OECD, OXFAM America, UNICEF and the Government of Senegal for supporting its research, training and publication programmes.

Contents

Chapter 1
The Public Sector and Administrative Reform

Chapter 2
The Politics of State Capacity Building in Africa: Issues and Challenges

Chapter 3
Theoretical Drivers of Public Sector Reform Initiatives in Africa

Chapter 4
Phases of Public Sector Reform in Africa

Chapter 5
Strategies of Public Sector Reform: The Balance Sheet

Contents

Chapter 6
The Future of the African Public Sector:
Alternative Approaches to Renewal and Reconstruction

Chapter 1

The Public Sector and Administrative Reform

Introduction

Since the late 1950s and 1960s, the public sector in most African states has generally been regarded as pivotal to promoting socio-economic development. The public sector comprises a number of institutions to make and implement decisions with regard to interests of various kinds. Its basic function was to provide goods and services to citizens based on the 'realization and representation of public interests and its possession of unique public qualities compared to business management' (Haque 2001: 65).

However, the public sector was not able to perform effectively because of 'accumulation of excessive power, lack of accountability and representation, indifference towards public needs and demands, official secrecy and inaccessibility, and role in depoliticizing the public sphere' (Haque 1994). This ineffectiveness, coupled with the economic crises of the late 1970s and 1980s, and apparent lessons from international experience of the success of market-friendly economies, have combined to produce, what some have referred to, as the 're-definition of the role of the state or public sector' (Fiszbein 2000:163).

The redefinition of the role of the state or the public sector[1] and the need to overhaul administrative systems and rejuvenate public organisations in both developed and developing countries cannot be over-emphasised:

> Though the dawn has been clouded and goals cannot be easily defined, the vitality of a country's development depends on the rejuvenation of public administration even in the darkness of insufficient knowledge and experience (Rizos 1965).

Public sector reforms in developed countries such as the UK, the US, Canada and Australia have shown that changes in political, social, economic and administrative environments, such as economic and fiscal crises of the state, the influence of neo-liberal ideas, such as public choice theory and criticisms of the old public administration, changes in political and ideological context, for example, ideas of the 'New Right', development in information technology, and the growth and role of management consultants have prompted and driven radical changes in public administration and management systems. The central objective of change was improvement in the ways in which government is managed and services delivered, with emphasis on effectiveness, efficiency, economy and value for money (Lane 1997; Kettl 1997; Metcalfe and Richards 1990).

In Africa and other developing countries, however, the need to reform public sector institutions has been prompted largely by worldwide decline in public finances and the need 'to get more for less' (Caiden 1988: 332). The unjust international economic system and persistent public pressures for increased government intervention to reverse the situation have forced governments in Africa and other developing countries to adopt temporary measures. These have resulted in large-scale borrowing, unprecedented public debt, high rates of inflation, frequent currency devaluations, and harsh policies imposed under the pressure of the World Bank and IMF (Hicks and Kubisch 1984). Governments have had to reduce expenditure on staff, investments and services, and to demand higher productivity and better performance from their sluggish public sectors.

In order to improve their countries' positions in the emerging world economy, governments in Africa and other developing countries have been forced to redefine their roles and strategies. In doing so, almost all have blamed the 'dead hand' of bureaucracy: the poor performance of public bureaucracies, the daily annoyances of irksome restrictions, cumbersome red tape, unpleasant officials, poor service and corrupt practices.[2] The 'dead hand' of bureaucracy was to be replaced by a new invigorating concept of public management and clear proof that public organisations were value for money (World Bank 1997a).

Against this background, this book examines reform of the public sector in Africa. It provides an overview of public sector reforms and implications for the future of a capable state. It draws on lessons about the concept of reform and public sector management. It begins by examining the concept of administrative reform, followed by a review of the literature on the factors that have driven reform of Africa's public sector. The major thrusts of the new administrative reform agenda devised by African countries are surveyed.

Defining the Public Sector and Its Scope

The public sector has become a commonplace term since the end of the second world war in 1945. Partly because of the expansion of governmental activity; and partly because it is associated with a socialist attitude to economic and social activity that is positive and directional, as distinct from the laissez-faire approach of individual self interest, which is conventionally associated with private enterprise. The public sector thus represents a group of institutions, which have in common some reliance on the power of the state, from which they can justify their activities; and a political belief which accords greater merit to collective over individual action (UN 1961; Thornhill 1985).

To define the public sector in institutional terms, we should be clear about the meaning of the term 'public'. In this study, it is simply used to imply the invocation of the power of the state. By extension, the public sector is deemed to comprise of bodies, the existence or powers of which rely on the authority conferred on them by the state, in varying degrees, through some formal process. Their ability to invoke, to a greater or lesser degree, the compulsive power of the state brings them within the public sector. In so far as that power exists, it is dealt with through recognised processes of political control in a democracy (United Nations 1961, 1975; Thornhill 1985).

The endowment of state power varies from one institution to another; though three broad groups can be identified. First are those bodies, which are readily recognisable, as obviously exercising governmental functions: ministries, departments, agencies, local government units and similar public bodies. These are clearly governmental bodies in the fullest sense, most with long histories (United Nations 1975; Fernandes 1986; Powell 1987).

Secondly, there are bodies such as state enterprises, boards and corporations, 'parastatals', such as electricity and water enterprises, the governmental sanction of which lies in the legislation which determines their institutional structure, finances, powers and duties; but whose external façade rests on long-established professional or technical personnel and practices, and which mainly began life as private ventures. Generally, the compulsive power inherent in this group relates to the enforcement of a monopoly or a sole duty. Their jurisdiction is limited to a particular area, as in the case of electricity corporations; or, to a particular service, such as railways. The institution may thus be a monopoly supplier of different kinds of services serving the same social or economic purpose. The provider of a sole duty is a monopoly of kind. A water corporation, in respect of environmental and sewage services, is such an example, in that it is the sole provider in its respective area of service, and is financed by public

3

money. It is the only body in that particular area providing services out of public funds; but it is not a monopolist in the true economic sense since there is competition from private suppliers (Pozen 1976; Fernandes 1986; Powell 1987).

Thirdly, there are many institutions whose activities concern citizens pursuing their individual personal interests, but which can enforce certain of their decisions by sanction of a governmental power conferred on them. The best examples of this group are professional regulatory bodies; in which state power is usually conferred to enable a body to have an ultimate enforcement role, considered to be of public benefit. Thus professional regulatory bodies are given the power to prescribe the training required for members; to regulate the conduct of members; and to prohibit the unqualified from practising. In a similar way, a number of bodies are endowed with compulsory powers to regulate various kinds of activities in the public interest (Pozen 1976; Fernandes 1986; Powell 1987).

The Public Sector in Development

The role of the public sector in national and regional development cannot be adequately discussed without reference to the impact of colonialism. At the political or administrative level, colonial policy, irrespective of the colonial power, left a legacy that created conditions to foster the development of highly personalised and leadership-dependent political systems prevalent in African countries (Wunsch 1995; Herbst 2000). Colonialism resulted in social fragmentation, economic backwardness and international vulnerability. Faced with these circumstances, African leaders reacted almost as a body, concluding that a massive, coordinated and nationally led attack on underdevelopment was necessary to bring about growth and poverty reduction. Given the array of challenges and problems they faced, African leaders' identification of capitalism with European colonialism led many to espouse socialism and reinforce a predictable orientation to centralised development (Lewis 1998; Chazan et al. 1992).

Furthermore, strong central government was regarded as essential to national unity, the modernisation of African states, and to counter internal social and ethnic fragmentation brought about by the policy of balkanisation of African states by the colonial powers, which had ignored ethnic and cultural factors in determining national boundaries. This option was not surprising for three reasons (Wunsch 1995a, 1995b). First, it was consistent with the structure and habits of the colonial-administrative state. Second, it was selected in an era when both Eastern and Western models of development emphasised central

4

direction and planning. Thirdly, it complemented the expectations of international assistance organisations for 'rational' planning, management and negotiation of assistance programmes. At the economic level, the centralising impact of colonialism is evidenced in the economic conditions most African states faced at independence. According to the World Bank:

> When the sub-Saharan states won independence...they faced formidable constraints to development. These included underdeveloped resources, political fragility, insecurely rooted and ill-suited institutions, a climate and geography hostile to development, and rapid population growth (World Bank 1981: 9).

In addition, colonialism reinforced centralism and elitism in the physical and human legacies it left. The administrative and supporting infrastructure – administrative headquarters, educational facilities, public utilities, consumer goods and communication facilities – was generally concentrated in a single city.

The colonial legacy of administration and governance gave birth to five complementary strategies, which were pursued by African leaders after independence, and thereafter until the 1980s, when structural adjustment programmes and conditions made them inapplicable. These can be summarised as: the replacement of competitive politics by one or no-party systems ostensibly dedicated to national unity; reliance upon unified bureaucratic structures exclusively accountable to the central government to define, organise, and manage the production of public goods and services along lines determined at all levels by a 'national plan'; that no legitimate significant role be allowed for local government, including traditional, ethnically related groups as well as modern institutions of true local government; executive authority to be maximised at the expense of such other institutions as the legislature, judiciary, regional governments, and press and private organisations; and that the national budget to be regarded as the primary source of funding for the development agenda, to be raised out of the largest economic sectors: either agriculture or mineral extraction (Wunsch 1995b).

Present-day African countries were created by colonial governments that often ignored ethnic and cultural factors in determining national boundaries. Colonially demarcated boundaries arbitrarily brought together diverse peoples within a single colonial territory. Under colonialism, ethnic and cultural feelings were stimulated, even sharpened. Administrative areas were often based along ethnic lines. Social and economic change was uneven. Some regions produced cash-crops and mineral products, while others lacked major natural resources. Missionary schools proliferated in some areas, while others received little exposure to Western-style education. At independence, African countries lacked a national identity. This was partly because colonial policy did much to strengthen ethnic (as opposed to national) consciousness; and partly because countries were too recent in existence to elicit a sense of common nationhood (Tivey 1981).

This legacy of colonialism has very important implications for African leadership. Colonialism was an alien imposition on African societies. It was authoritarian by nature and usually distant from its subjects. At the same time, colonial administration was often thin on the ground. There was no intensive bureaucratic presence in many of the territories. While colonial authorities did exercise stable rule and provided some basic public goods, their subjects viewed them as illegitimate and predatory (Chazan et al. 1992).

The colonial inheritance created basic problems for the establishment of effective government during the post-independence period. African leaders faced manifold difficulties in gathering stable governing coalitions, fostering durable institutions and extending substantial control over the majority populations. Emergent government formulae typically blended traditional modes of authority with institutional forms inherited from the colonial regime. These strategies often stabilised nascent political elites, yet they were less effective in building sound governing structures.

Consequently, colonialism presented African leaders with three formidable challenges to development. First, the project of state-building. African countries have faced difficulties in constructing effective public authority, establishing viable state institutions and creating responsive and legitimate agents of governance. Attaining security and managing conflict are integral features of state consolidation. Building public power requires much more than the installation of new governmental structures. Indeed, it involves the very character of relations between rulers and ruled (Chazan et al. 1992; Hyden 1983).

The second challenge posed to African leaders was the task of nation-building. Many African countries have experienced the travails of forging unified political communities from plural states. Because of the arbitrary basis of colonial boundaries, newly independent states inherited diverse populations that often became fractious as disparate groups contended for resources and identity. The difficulties of managing competition and strife among ethnic communities and promoting common symbols and identifies have placed substantial demands upon governments throughout the region (Hyden 1983; Lewis 1998).

A third overarching task for African leaders is economic development. Leaders have had to cope with the myriad challenges of growth and structural transformation in low-income agrarian economies. They have also grappled with external dependence and a marginal position in world markets, where commodity prices are subject to fluctuations, over which they have no control or input. Leaders have pursued various programmes without successfully promoting a diversified production base, or making inroads against poverty and inequality (Lewis 1998; Chazan et al. 1992; Ayee 2001).

Given these challenges, and the role of the state in socio-economic development, the ends of the modern state were revolutionised, and the purposes of the public sector completely reoriented. The public sector was no longer the preserver of the status quo, rather it was expected to be the accelerator of economic and social change. In its new role as the prime mover and stimulator of national development, it was expected to spread the benefits of economic and social progress to everyone, not only the privileged few.

Moreover, the public sector was expected to achieve these purposes within the general framework of the consent of the people, with due regard for the rule of law and individual human rights. It is difficult to find a state that does not call itself a democracy: a government of the people, irrespective of its present power structure (United Nations 1961).

The functions of the modern state, consequentially of public administration, were new, both in their dynamism, and in their universality. There are no limits on the services, which the state is called on to provide. Countries, which in the nineteenth century, achieved politically democratic forms and instituted a number of social services have in the twentieth century greatly expanded their activities in economic and social fields.

There are evidently great variations in the functions assumed by the public sector. These grew out of dissimilar national traditions and philosophies, and from great disparities in national resources and methods of utilising them. The public sector may act as the director, entrepreneur or stimulator of private initiative, or in all three capacities. In a socialist state, practically all organised effort is placed in the public sector. Its entire management becomes the concern of public service.

Many countries, for reasons dictated by history, philosophy and resources are committed to reserving the largest possible sphere of activity to private enterprise and local initiative. But even in these countries, vastly increased functions have been given to the public sector. Thus developed economies, such as the UK and US, have witnessed a great expansion of their public services. The governments of such countries have undertaken new tasks in the regulation, stimulation, coordination and financing of independent and local centres of initiative.

They have created new services under their public administrations in many fields where private capital is unable to enter (Thornhill 1985).

The twentieth century has witnessed an unprecedented extension of governmental functions. The concept of the service and welfare state has been almost universally accepted. The public sector has taken on itself responsibility for the direction and utilisation of manpower, natural resources and the fast-growing technology of the modern world for the creation of an environment conducive to widespread economic and social well-being. Citizens make insistent demands upon the public sector, increasingly rejecting lives of poverty, hunger, disease and ignorance. More and more, particularly in developing countries, the public sector is looked on as the agency to meet these urgent demands, and to devise new forms of public administration to overcome social and economic deficiencies (Lane 1993).

Braibant (1996:163-176) summarised the role of the public sector in development as follows. First, the public sector is responsible for the regulation of economic life. Contrary to a widespread belief, a market economy system does not reduce the need for regulation. On the contrary, it increases the need. Regulation is essential, as it prevents competitive distortions and the misuse of positions of prominence. It protects workers and consumers, and prevents markets becoming jungles ruled by the survival of the fittest. Indeed, captains of industry themselves, in spite of an attachment to market freedoms, call upon the state to obtain assistance, for example, with investments or exports.

Second, the public sector plays a unique part in ensuring social cohesion. Only the public sector or the state can guarantee equality of opportunity, combat social inequalities and protect the weak in the areas of education, health and housing. In periods of crisis, only the state can implement the necessary measures to reduce unemployment to an acceptable level, or eliminate an explosive situation caused by abject poverty or the exclusion of certain segments of the population.

The public sector controls international migration flows. It ensures the integration of foreigners within the national community, the protection of minorities and the safeguarding of law and order in complex, multiethnic and multicultural societies.

The public sector is involved in town and country planning, nature conservation, and the safeguarding of historical and cultural heritage and scientific research. It has responsibility for the relationships between cities, rural districts and various regions of the national territory. It assumes responsibility for solidarity between generations and sustainable development. While sharing its responsibilities with civic society, the public sector acts to safeguard and manage the collective memory of a country, and prepare its future. It is thus responsible for safeguarding checks and balances: fundamental elements in complex societies.

In short, the public sector has an enormous impact on the entire public through a set of hierarchical structures that are responsive to politicians. Politicians are supposed to take care of the normative side of things and pursue public interests. Effective bureaucracies are supposed to ensure that goals are implemented (Lane 1993).

The Concept of Administrative Reform

The theoretical basis structuring these chapters is the concept of administrative reform. The reasoning determining this approach is that most strategies or devices employed by African countries to reform their public sectors such as decentralisation, privatisation, commercialisation, contracting out and public-private partnership are all predicated on the concept of administrative reform.

Defining Administrative Reform

There are numerous definitions of administrative reform. Some focus on political interactions of stakeholders, which actually determine the course of events. For instance, Caiden (1969: 65) defines administrative reform as 'the artificial inducement of administrative transformation, against resistance', which contains three interrelated concepts: moral purpose: the need to improve on the status quo; artificial transformation: departure from existing arrangements and natural change processes; and administrative resistance, where opposition is assumed.

Other definitions focus on reform as containing elements of rational instrumentality. There is an assumption that reformers have accurate knowledge of cause and effect. In this regard, Dror defines reform as 'directed change of main features of an administrative system'; and as containing two properties: goal orientation (directed, conscious) and the comprehensiveness of change (number of administrative components affected, state of change) (Dror 1976: 127).

This is not a departure from the United Nations (1973: 2) definition of reform as 'specially designed efforts to induce fundamental changes in public administration systems through system-wide reforms or at least through measures for improvement of one or more of its key elements, distinct from normal and containing administration and management improvement in terms of their scope, modus operandi and implications'.

Some scholars emphasise the outcomes of administrative reform by identifying it as the means 'to make the administrative system a more effective instrument for social change, a better instrument to bring about political equality, social justice and economic growth' (Samonte 1970: 288). Others focus on process. For example, Kahn (1981) sees reform as changing established bureaucratic practices, behaviours and structures. Quah (1976) and Jreisat (1988) incorporate multiple views by linking processual changes to the production of a more effective and efficient bureaucracy. Quah, for example, sees reform as a deliberate attempt to change both the structure and procedures of the public bureaucracy, i.e. reorganisation, or the institutional aspect; and also the attitudes and behaviour of the public bureaucrats involved, i.e. the attitudinal aspect, in order to promote organisational effectiveness and attain national development goals (Quah 1976: 58).

In spite of the different definitions, there are certain common elements of administrative reform including: deliberate plans to change public bureaucracies; administrative reform being anonymous with innovation: the injection of new ideas and new people in a new combination of tasks and relationships into the policy and administrative process; improvement in public service effectiveness and efficiency; and coping with uncertainties and rapid changes taking place in the organisational environment (de Guzman and Reforma 1992; Turner and Hulme 1997).

Strategies of Administrative Reform

Turner and Hulme (1997), Peters (1992), Dror (1976), Caiden (1978, 1991) and Peters (1992) have identified a number of strategies that have been employed in administrative reform.

Restructuring. This involves the redesigning of the structure of organisations to improve effectiveness and efficiency. Restructuring devices include eliminating red tape, downsizing, decentralising authority, and improving organisational effectiveness through privatisation, commercialisation, partnerships and co-production. The reform agenda usually includes an attempt to address the rigidities and dysfunctions associated with mechanical structures, a process referred to as 'de-bureaucratisation' (Turner and Hulme 1997; Caiden 1978, 1991).

Human Resource Issues. The reform of human resources focuses on human resource development (HRD) and human resource management (HRM). This is important because an organisation's most valuable resources are its staff, which perform and coordinate tasks, organise inputs and produce outputs. Hence HRM and HRD are crucial for reformers aiming at greater efficiency and effectiveness in public bureaucracies.

While HRM focuses on selection, recruitment, appraisal, reward and career opportunities within an organisation, HRD refers to the organisational activities directed at improving the skills and capacities of the workforce. Taken together, HRM and HRD are seen as principal means of promoting improvements in organisational capacity — a highly favoured and oft-repeated objective of administrative reform.

Human resource (HR) initiatives in developed and developing countries include: increasing emphasis on training and the development of interpersonal skills; providing career advice and mentoring; encouragement of mobility and broadening experience; introducing participative management styles; providing performance feedback; introducing human resource planning systems; human resource development planning; devolution of personnel management functions and power; management training; and remuneration (EDI and ISAS 1992; Peters 1992; Dror 1976).

Participation. Participation involves reforms aimed at decentralisation, thereby providing greater scope for continuing participation in significant decision-making, by both organisational members and clients of the organisation. Perceived advantages of participation include a lesser need for coordination and control, more effective utilisation of human resources, greater commitment to organisational objectives, and public intervention in shaping the activities of public bureaucracies in order to provide services that are both required and desired (Turner and Hulme 1997; Peters 1992).

Accountability. Accountability is one of the most important objectives of public sector reforms. In the words of Paul (1991: 5), accountability is the 'driving force that generates the pressure for key actors involved to be responsible for and to ensure good public service performance'. It involves not only tackling corruption, but also improving public sector performance, effectiveness, efficiency, achievement of goals, probity and regularity on the part of public officials who are expected to follow formal rules and regulations. A range of institutions has been created to promote accountability, including auditors and ombudspersons. A key question remains: to whom is the public servant accountable? (Paul 1992). *Public-Private Sector Partnerships.* Donor agencies drive privatisation and commercialisation, co-production and deregulation. They also emphasise and encourage public-private sector synergy or partnership in the provision of social welfare, public goods and services. Such partnerships or cooperation are meant to present governments with the opportunities to improve citizen access to services. In addition, the competition in such service provision arrangements is expected to encourage quality institutions (Batley 1994, 1997; Collins 2000).

Literature Review of the Factors Influencing Public Sector Reform in Africa

This literature review of administrative reforms is divided into sections on developed and African countries.

Literature on Administrative Reform in Developed Countries

This literature indicates that changes in socio-economic conditions in the 1970s and 1980s provided grounds for administrative reforms in the socio-economic reforms in both developed and developing countries (Caiden 1969, 1976, 1978, 1988, 1991; Bjur and Caiden 1978; Boudiguel and Rouban 1988).

These administrative reforms were partly prompted by the worldwide economic recession of the 1970s and 1980s. They de-emphasised the role of the state in favour of the private sector in the socio-economic life of countries concerned. This phenomenon was referred to as 'rolling back the state', or 'withdrawal of the state'.

Underpinning these reforms was a search for efficiency and effectiveness in the face of dwindling resources (World Bank 1997). They were elaborated in most cases into a general crusade to reorganise and modernise the public sector, including the civil service (Caiden 1973, 1988, 1991; Dror 1976; Peters 1992; Collins 2000).

These changes have their political and ideological underpinnings in the rise of neoliberal economic thinking and conservatism in both the UK and US in the late 1970s and 1980s. They were reflected in the concurrent shift in the strategies of the IMF and the World Bank towards a more liberal market-oriented ideology (Christensen 1988; Luke 1991; Collins 2000).

Implications for public services included demands for a smaller but more efficient and effective public service. In the process of reforms, management techniques from the private sector were imported into the public service such as 'programme, planning and budgeting systems' (PPBS), performance-related pay, 'management by objectives' (MBO) and contract-based appointments (Batley 1994).

The emergence of the neoliberal agenda in the form of 'rolling-back the state' in Western countries in the 1970s began to find expression in the economic reform programmes supported by the IMF and World Bank in African countries in the 1980s. Here, there was a similar demand for smaller, efficient and cost-effective public administration institutions, which could only be achieved through reforms.

Literature on Administrative Reform in African Countries

This literature can be broadly cast into two sections: studies from general public administration and development administration fields that have contributed to administrative reforms under structural adjustment programmes (SAPs); and studies that have specifically studied SAP-related public service reforms.

The first category includes the corporate works of the African Training Centre for Administration and Development (CAFRAD) (1990), Balogun and Mutahaba (1991), and the individual works of Mutahaba (1989), Adamolekun (1991), Kaul (1996), Macgregor et al. (1998) and Olowu (1999). These studies highlight the general impact of SAPs on public sector institutions. They cover a variety of issues from privatisation and deregulation, through decentralisation and civil service reforms, to problems confronting the public service in Africa, such as serious human resource leadership management issues; performance-related pay; related governance reforms; and appropriate strategy for mobilising resources. It is pointed out that these issues must be adequately addressed before African countries can make significant progress in the public sector and development.

CAFRAD's work was pioneering in its responses to the implications and the impact of SAPs on public administration structures and management. Some of the important issues raised in CAFRAD's work are set out below.

Firstly, administrative reforms in Africa resulted from a serious economic crisis. They were thus not ends in themselves; rather directed at supporting policies for economic stabilisation and adjustment. Consequently these administrative reforms sometimes failed to answer the specific needs of African countries.

Secondly, the central objectives of SAP-related administrative reforms were to reduce costs and increase the effectiveness of public services. Reduction in the size of the public service, including the civil service, as a requirement of SAP, was based on the goal of reducing budget deficits and redressing financial imbalances. This contrasts with the additional demands that the implementation of SAPs imposed on the public sector, such as the requirement to produce voluminous information and data aimed at monitoring the implementation of structural adjustment.

Most of the contributions in the volume edited by Balogun and Mutahaba (1991) dwell on the effects of the economic crisis on public sector institutions, rather than the impact of SAPs on these institutions. There is a distinction between the effects of the crisis on the one hand, and the effects of adjustment on the other. It is to be expected that any SAP-related administrative reforms would seek to redress some of the negative impacts of the crisis on the public services in general, and on the civil service in particular.

A few of the contributions in Balogun and Mutahaba (1991) do however focus on the impact of SAPs on the public service. Adamolekun, for instance, highlights the World Bank's involvement in public sector management improvements in Africa. He notes that improvement of civil service management under adjustment programmes involves: staff reduction, salary and wage reviews, and the strengthening and reorganisation of key ministries and central agencies in some African countries such as the Gambia, Senegal and Mali.

Wamalwa, in the same volume, argues that SAPs have promoted cost-consciousness at all levels of the public administration system. They have the potential to ensure merit-based employment and the rationalisation of public administration institutions, such as the public and civil services. However, concomitant restrictions on employment and the mass retrenchment of public sector personnel have had adverse effects on motivation, morale and productivity (Balogun and Mutahaba 1991: 109-19).

Writing on administrative reforms in East Africa, Mutahaba (1989) has noted that many of the reform efforts in Tanzania, Zambia and Kenya took place amidst complementary reforms in socio-economic systems. In most cases, in these three countries, administrative reform measures were taken to facilitate socio-economic development objectives. In agreement with the CAFRAD study (1990) and Nti (1991), Mutahaba argues forcefully that reform efforts should not be concerned merely with rehabilitating the public service systems. Rather, they should aim at transforming and building viable systems capable of handling the shocks of independence and economic crisis.

A few studies have focused specifically on adjustment-related public sector reforms, notably de Merode writing for the United Nations (1992), Olowu (1999), Demongeot (1994), Macgregor (1998), Wescott (1999), Kaul (1996) and Langseth (1995). De Merode (1992) outlines two sets of reasons that have been used to justify the reform of the public sector under structural adjustment. Firstly, most of the Africa public services were oversized, thus placing a budgetary burden on the government, especially in the context of economic decline and increasing budget deficits. An obvious way to redress the imbalance was to reduce the number and cost of public servants, a prominent feature of SAPs.

The second set of reasons justifying SAP-related public sector reforms have to do with weak government capacities, reflected in weak public sector capacities. These represent bottlenecks for both the immediate feasibility and the long-term sustainability of SAPs. Public service reform was therefore required for the effective implementation of structural adjustment.

However, works of the United Nations (1992), Olowu (1999), Demongeot (1994), Macgregor (1998), Wescott (1999), Kaul (1996), and Langseth (1995) differ in position from that of de Merode. While recognising that public sector reforms were overdue in African countries, and that some African public services were oversized, ineffective and inefficient, they express doubt as to whether SAPs provide a basis for comprehensive administrative reforms in the public service. In particular, they emphasise that reduction in the size of the public service and cost-cutting, privatisation and deregulation would not necessarily improve the efficiency and effectiveness of the public sector, unless attention is focused on other aspects of public service management, such as capacity building, service delivery, aid mechanisms, change management processes, leadership commitment, sequencing, ministerial restructuring, decentralisation, attitudinal changes, change in perception and good governance.

Two conclusions may be drawn from this review. First, major socio-economic reforms, such as those introduced under structural adjustment, would require capable administrative machinery to support and sustain them. For most African countries, this would imply comprehensive and system-wide reforms in the public service. However, the literature suggests that reforms have been less comprehensive and systemic in their impacts.

Secondly, it may be concluded that public sector reforms are a by-product of structural adjustment programmes. This implies that the scope and content of the reforms have been largely determined by adjustment conditions.

The Structural or Institutional Approach

The constitution of the public sector, the concept of administrative reform and different approaches to the question of reform have been discussed. It is pertinent at this stage to articulate the approach that is being used to conduct this analysis, and reasons for this choice.

The approach adopted in the book is the structural or institutional approach. The focus of the approach is the uniqueness of institutions and structures, both in time and place. Institutions embody cultures and past political decisions. Formal rules and structures, agreed or introduced long ago, influence how political actors exercise their current choices. In the words of John (2002: 40): 'It is the variety of traditions embodied in institutions that explains the complexity of political behaviour and unlocks the intricacies of the policy process.'

It is instructive to note that institutions and structures have taken a central and particular place in the origins of the discipline of political science, because they define how a political system operates. The founding scholars of political science treated institutions such as the executive, legislatures, bureaucracies and courts as key components of public life, worthy of study in their own right. Their importance was reinforced by the significance of institutions in the classic works of political theorists such as Alexis de Tocqueville, and in the *Federalist Papers* (Madison et al. 1788).

Institutions and structures are regarded as the arena within which public policy making takes place. They include political organisations, laws and rules that are central to every political system. Institutions constrain how decision makers behave. They divide power and responsibilities between the organisations of the state. They confer rights on individuals and groups, and impose obligations on state officials to consult and to deliberate. And they can conclude and exclude political actors, including civil society organisations (CSOs), in public policy making. Not only do institutions affect the distribution of power, they also render political life manageable by formalising rules and norms of behaviour (Weaver 1993; March and Olsen 1976).

Structural or institutional approaches have been criticised for being descriptive and obsessed with administrative detail and formal procedures. It is also true that actors and groups often circumvent institutions in the pursuit of their interests. Nevertheless, this approach is being used here for a number of reasons.

First, institutions affect the power of groups, shape the way ideas circulate to influence policy, and influence the coordination of public policies. As well as being the formal apparatus of government, the profound and subtle influence of institutions stems from their role in comprising the norms and conventions of behaviour (March and Olsen 1989).

Secondly, institutions are habits of decision making and belief systems. They are embedded within the institutional framework, which in turn affects the power of groups in the policy process. Indeed, institutions are resistant to change. Hence they are an independent factor affecting political behaviour (John 2002; March and Olsen 1989). Since reforming the public service in Africa involves norms and conventions of behaviour and formalised procedure, as well as the role of different institutions and structures in both inter and intra policy sectors, the structural or institutional approach represents an appropriate tool with which to conduct the analysis.

Chapter 2

The Politics of State Capacity Building in Africa: Issues and Challenges

Introduction

The terms 'state' and 'public sector' have been used synonymously because there can be no strong state without an efficient public sector (African Development Bank 2005). However for purposes of analysis, and to contextualise reform of the African public sector and understand its processes, dynamics and intricacies, it is pertinent to examine the state and state capacity building in Africa. This chapter therefore considers the postcolonial state in Africa, and efforts to build its capacity.

It is noteworthy that the postcolonial state in Africa has attracted interest in three thematic areas: state consolidation; state decline; and state capacity building.

State consolidation, which came into vogue in the immediate post-independence era, emanated from the underlying assumption that the state was a major means of bringing about societal change and fulfilling economic and social aspirations, with strong integrative and development objectives (Herbst 2000).

The shift to state decline from the mid-1970s focuses on analysing what went wrong with the state, and reasons for its weakness. The state proved incapable of bringing about intended changes in society. It was considered built on doubtful foundations of legitimacy. The state was variously characterised as 'prismatic' (Riggs 1964), 'soft' (Myrdal 1968), 'weak' (Jackson and Rosberg 1982), 'overdeveloped' (Leys 1976), as a 'precapitalist affectation' (Hyden 1983) and 'anti-development' (Dwivedi and Nef 1982), because of its inability to meet the aspirations not only of civil society but also of those who occupied central political institutions (Azarya 1988).

This characterisation was a major cause of the economic decline experienced by most African countries during the 1970s and 1980s. Furthermore, it weakened government capacity and effectiveness, which in turn hindered economic revival efforts via structural adjustment (Jeffries 1993).

Given the incapacity of the state to implement structural adjustment programmes, in the 1980s, the World Bank and other donors moved towards concern with improving state capacity, through 'rolling back the state'. This meant restricting the role of the state, while providing greater opportunity for market forces to assert themselves on the development process, and liberalising the economy with the hope of inducing economic development.

This approach also involves building administrative capacity as an instrument of the development process, rather than as a spoils system, and the development of more efficient and, in some senses, more autonomous state machines. Various panaceas were suggested, including administrative reform covering areas such as organisational and manpower development, training, and the introduction of management techniques along the lines of the 'New Public Management' school (Schaffer 1969; Levy 2004; Haque 2001).

Strategies of Administration and Governance

Two strategies of administration and governance have emerged in Africa since independence: political and personal concerns of the leaders, and 'neo-patrimonialism'. These strategies have led to African leaders pursuing short-term destructive policies and programmes, especially in the economic sector.

Political and Personal Concerns of Leaders

Unlike East Asian state elites of the same period, who are perceived as having been strongly oriented towards developmental goals, African post-independence elites appear to have been motivated more by political and personal concerns than by economic and social development. After independence, African leaders were concerned with the twin objectives of remaining in power and building an economic base for themselves. The desire to hold on to power was not simply driven by a lust for power itself. Many of the triumphant nationalist leaders saw themselves as 'unique liberators of their people who deserved unlimited tenure to rule their newly independent countries' (Tangri 1999: 9).

But power also brought with it many opportunities for attaining wealth in an African context of extreme scarcity and poverty, with limited means of private accumulation. To be in key administrative and political positions was to have access to the major means of acquiring coveted material resources. This was particularly relevant as states were accorded such a dominant role in post-independence national economies. Through the state, top officeholders controlled extensive arrays of resources. They could influence tier distribution and accumulation, often with an eye to political advantage as well as personal gain. Other avenues to wealth, such as through the private economy, were more restricted, especially as the larger private enterprises were in non-African hands; and an indigenous capitalist class was weakly developed. Thus political office in sub-Saharan Africa assumed major significance.

Not surprisingly therefore, political power became the site of intense struggle. Nearly everywhere, desperate struggles ensued to attain or maintain state power. In the words of Bratton and van de Walle (1997: 119) right up until the first half of the 1990s, 'the most common path of regime transition was liberalization without democratization'.

Those in power have employed diverse measures to remain there, including intimidation and repression of political opponents. Post-independence African governments have commonly resorted to various authoritarian means to retain power. Postcolonial states have resurrected the many autocratic practices of one-party systems, in which a single ruler or a small oligarchy possess almost unrestricted power. Given the weakness of civil societies, social forces have been unable to counterbalance state dominance. Centralised power and personalised rule have prevailed in most African countries. Recent years have seen some degree of political liberalisation: multiparty elections, fewer restrictions on the media, and more assertive legislatures in most of sub-Saharan Africa. However, personalistic and authoritarian political practices still enable incumbent rulers to impede full political competition, as well as to maintain themselves in power (Clapham 1985; Sandbrook 1985; Tordoff 1985; Bratton and Hyden 1992; Ayee 2001).

Neo-Patrimonialism

Besides authoritarianism, an important, non-coercive form of consolidating power has been to rely on patronage. To secure political incumbency, public benefits and opportunities have been distributed along political lines. Thus, in their quest for self-preservation, state elites have dispensed government-controlled resources — jobs, licenses, contracts and credit — to select political allies. They have mediated access to economic opportunities in favour of close associates, so as to enhance their hold over state power.

In Africa, ethnic identities have comprised the key basis on which clientelistic coalitions have been built. Political leaders have allocated public resources and amenities to key intermediaries and their ethnic clienteles in ways designed to fashion a following and ensure political support. As a result, most regimes have been identified with specific ethnic and regional interests, although many have simultaneously been able to consolidate their hold on state power for long periods by promoting relatively ethnically balanced distribution of government resources (Tangri 1999; Bratton and Hyden 1992).

In order to enhance the patronage resources available for distribution, Africa's new rulers 'extended the scope of direct government-involvement in the economy'. They 'expanded the public sector of the economy', and thereby 'multiplied opportunities for patronage and clientelism, and allowed regimes to channel economic resources to targeted social groups' (Boone 1992: 16 -17). Politically mediated access to resources and economic opportunities controlled by the state became key mechanisms of consolidating power. To be sure, resources available to the state have, at times, markedly decreased; as, for example, in the cases of Zambia and Zaire where copper prices collapsed from the mid-1970s. Moreover, the economic reform programmes from mid-1980s, initiated by the Bretton Wood institutions, brought cuts in state spending and reductions in the public benefits in exchange for political support. Nevertheless, African political leaders have continued to use the state and its resources to maintain themselves in power. In the words of Tangri (1999: 11):

Patronage politics has been integral to post-colonial efforts to maintain political control in poor, ethnically diverse peasant societies. Yet, although valuable in helping to consolidate ruling coalitions, the dynamics of patronage relations have proved economically highly damaging.

Economic management of the state has taken place in a special governance environment, based largely on patronage networks coupled with a virtual absence of scrutiny over public resource allocation. This logic of patrimonialism has shaped the economic actions of top politicians and administrators who run largely authoritarian regimes. But as Sandbrook (1985: 19) notes, patrimonialism is 'potentially economically destructive'. In Africa, 'its short-term political rationality of personal and regime survival' has generated a 'variety of economic irrationalities that smother capitalism's expansive dynamics' (Sandbrook 1993: 27, 34). Top public sector positions, especially in important government ministries and key parastatals, have often been filled by politically loyal officials. The distribution of public services and economic infrastructure are attributable to a markedly patrimonial administration (Bratton and Hyden 1992).

21

It is important to note that because state institutions in Africa are fragile and command only limited public acceptance, informal networks of personal relationships emerge in society, to link a relatively powerful and well-placed patron with less powerful clients for the purpose of advancing their mutual interests. Patron-client ties have constituted the primary means of maintaining power in Africa. State elites have thus used public institutions to dispense an array of public benefits—jobs, credit, contracts, subsidies—to select clients and ethnic constituencies to build political support and consolidate themselves in state power in an authoritarian context in which they have rarely been held accountable for their actions (Tangri 1999).

The State, the Market and Public Purpose in Africa

Before dealing with state intervention in Africa, it is important to understand the motivation for public ownership, in Africa and other developing countries.

Motivation for Public Ownership

Public ownership serves a variety of political, economic and social objectives. Because of the different emphasis placed on these objectives, the size and structure of the public sector differs widely between countries. Firstly, from an economic viewpoint, the main arguments in favour of public ownership relate to the failure of markets to secure economic and social objectives. A major concern has been the inevitable tendency of certain markets toward monopoly, especially when technological factors imply that only one producer—a natural monopoly—can fully exploit available economies of scale. Such a situation typically emerges when heavy investment in a network, for example an electricity grid or a railway, is required.

Telecommunications and broadcasting systems have also tended to be regarded as natural monopolies, although recent rapid technological progress in these areas make this less justified. In other words, under certain conditions, 'the market produces suboptimal economic outcomes such as low production and extremes of wealth and poverty' (Nellis and Shirley 1991: 1).

Secondly, public ownership gives government the freedom to pursue objectives that the market would otherwise ignore. Most important among these are the goals of social equity, such as access to essential goods and services at an affordable price, and employment. A significant proportion of welfare economics is devoted to establishing the case for government intervention, though not necessarily public ownership, to regulate natural monopolies and meet compelling social needs (Hemming and Mansoor 1988).

Thirdly, government intervention is justified by the presence of external costs and benefits. The pursuit of social objectives often involves an effort to capture positive externalities (Bennell 1997). Governments hoped that public ownership of enterprises would assist the development of 'strategic' sectors, enable them to gain access to commercial credit that would be denied to small private businesses, fill 'entrepreneurial gaps', empower numerically large but economically weak segments of the population, maintain employment levels, and raise the level of savings and investment (the private sector, it was assumed, would consume wastefully, or remit its earnings abroad). Public ownership, it was thought, would not offer any inherent obstacles to the efficient functioning of these enterprises ((Nellis and Shirley 1991).

Fourthly, the weakness, or foreign dominance, or 'incorrect' ethnic composition of the indigenous private sector led many governments, especially in developing countries, to create alternative, large state-owned industrial enterprises (Bennell 1997).

While the boundary between the public and private sectors can in principle be defined by reference to efficiency and equity considerations, the diversity of experience between countries reflects the fact that a number of other factors – economic, political and strategic – must be taken into account. Indeed, the differences in motivation for public ownership are so varied that it is virtually impossible to systematically explain inter-country differences in the extent of public ownership. It is clear, however, that dissatisfaction with the public sector, and public enterprises in particular, is broad based. The source of this dissatisfaction is not solely ideological. There is now widespread doubt as to whether the benefits of public ownership are worth the cost (Hemming and Mansoor 1988).

Reasons Underlying State Intervention in Africa

Several studies have identified three main reasons for state intervention in the economy in Africa: statist conceptions of development; economic nationalism; and political patronage (Tangri 1999; Young 1991; Grosh and Mukandala 1994; Bennell 1997; Ramanadham 1995; Rondinelli and Lacono 1996; Haile-Mariam and Mengistu 1988; Kumssa 1996). These are explored below.

Statist Conceptions of Development

The African post-independence period in the 1960s, when the public sector was seen as a major contributor to economic growth and socio-political stability, witnessed an enormous expansion of government intervention in national economies. This statism, or state capitalism – ownership and intervention by the state – was accepted as the dominant development strategy and paradigm. The state had a central role to play in directing the development process. This was especially acknowledged in the African context of a weakly developed indigenous private sector, with substantial foreign economic presence. Thus justifying state intervention in the economy was a historical as well an ideological necessity. Consequently, various forms of state economic intervention, inherited from the colonial period, were expanded and generalised in the years after independence, leading, in particular, to the marked expansion of state owned enterprises undertaking important shares of production and investment in African countries (Tangri 1999; Young 1991; Bennell 1997).

Economic Nationalism or Africanisation of the Economy

After independence, there were strong feelings in Africa of 'economic nationalism'. This stemmed from the weakness and subordinate status of African private enterprise, as well as from the fact that African economies were largely in the hands of foreigners. Public sector enterprise was seen as enabling the state to carry out activities that African private entrepreneurs could not perform, and reduce the dominance of foreign enterprise. Throughout the continent, political leaders sought to secure greater indigenous ownership of the economy, especially of the activities on which a country depended for foreign exchange earnings. Greater ownership and control of the economy, through what was called 'capturing the commanding heights of the economy', to influence the broad direction of national development through the nationalisation of foreign economic concerns was enacted in Zambia, Tanzania, Nigeria, Ghana and Zimbabwe. In addition, new state owned enterprises were created in Swaziland and Kenya to accelerate the policy of 'Africanisation' of the economy. In such socialist countries as Tanzania, Ethiopia and Mozambique, the policy of extensive proliferation of state enterprises was pursued as a way of fulfilling ideological ambitions of governments (Ramanadham 1995; Rondinelli and Iacono 1996; Haile-Mariam and Mengistu 1988; Kumssa 1996; Adamolekun 1999).

Political Patronage

State intervention maintained leaders in power. The public enterprise sector offered leaders the resources and opportunities to meet some of the demands owing to intense pressures exerted on African leaders to provide employment and redistribute public resources. As a result, state owned enterprises (SOEs) had to be physically impressive, and spread all over the country. They were supposed to create new jobs and benefit the consumer via lower prices. Just as it was necessary to impress the electorate, it was also necessary to reward party activists. Hence the enterprises were used as sources of political patronage (Ayee 1990, 1994b; Grosh and Mukandala 1994).

This point has been reinforced by van de Walle, who argued that in Cameroon, SOEs 'proved to be an ideal instrument to distribute state resources in the form of jobs, rents, power and prestige which enabled President Ahmadou Ahidjo to reward allies and co-opt opponents and thus secure his power base' (van de Walle 1994: 155-6). In short, SOEs were beneficial to state officeholders in terms of consolidating their power and maintaining their political incumbency (Tangri 1999).

Furthermore, the creation of SOEs stemmed from the fact that they were visible and highly ostentatious evidence of governments' efforts to develop a country's economy. SOEs erected impressive facades: even though there was not much behind these in real terms, their political impact was considerable (Ayee 1986; Glentworth 1973).

Building State Capacity

State intervention in African economies has been largely viewed as counterproductive and detrimental to economic growth and progress. The period of state intervention came to be characterised by patronage, neo-patrimonialism, corruption, nepotism, inappropriate policy design, poor policy implementation and transactional rather than transformational leadership. None of these approaches were concerned with pursuing the public interest; but rather with sectional and partisan interests, poor service provision and delivery.

The economic crises which faced most African states in the 1970s and 1980s were coupled with the lessons of market forces in developed countries. The result was the need to redefine the role of the state through the building of its capacity.

Four features underpinned state capacity building: a reduction of the role of the state in national economic management; an enhanced role for sub-national governments; public-private partnership with respect to the production and provision of goods and services; and efforts such as designing corporate plans and signing of performance contracts aimed at achieving improved performance in public management (Adamolekun 1999).

Literature Review of State Capacity in Africa

The review of the literature on state capacity can be divided into the following thematic areas: the drivers of interest in state capacity; strategies and phases of modernisation of the state and their balance sheet; and, contextual variables affecting state capacity.

Drivers of Interest in State Capacity

There is evidence in the literature that interest in state capacity in Africa is attributable to four influences: the introduction of structural adjustment programmes in the mid-1980s; the good governance agenda of the late 1980s; the 'developmental state' idea; and the 'New Public Management' approach.

The Introduction of Structural Adjustment Programmes

The disastrous showing of statist policy in regulating the economy largely led to Africa's precipitous economic decline, which began in the late 1970s and early 1980s. Accordingly, African economic and political systems were influenced by donor nations, and, especially, by the World Bank and IMF. Stabilisation and structural adjustment programmes have been applied to the economies of developing countries with the support, or insistence, of these institutions. In many respects they have provided the framework within which other donor agencies operate. Among the main elements of their programmes have been the liberalisation of external trade and exchange rate policies, the elimination of governmental control of internal prices, and the reduction of the scale of the public sector in its role as a producer of goods and services (DeLancey 2001).

Structural adjustment has been associated with donor pressure to introduce new approaches to public sector management, aiming to replicate some of the claimed efficiencies of the private sector. It has included measures to create quasi market conditions in public service delivery, through the introduction of user charges and fees for cost recovery in social and infrastructural services – with widely disputed impacts on social distribution; exposure of public operators to private competition; the introduction of performance measurement and reward into public service employment conditions; and strengthening managerial au-

26

tonomy by devolving responsibilities for service delivery either to budget centres within an organisation or to semi-autonomous public agencies (Campbell and Loxley 1989).

However, the outcome of structural adjustment in African countries was not encouraging, because the reform depended on ready markets for exports and substantial investments from industrial countries, which, for the most part, were not substantiated. In the circumstances, economic stagnation and decline continued in most African states throughout the 1990s and first decades of the twenty-first century.

The systematic weakness of implementing adjustment packages suggests that understanding the roots of policy choices in Africa is more important than recommending the adoption of specific policies without understanding their context (Englebert 2000).

The Governance Agenda

Since the late 1980s the issue of governance has dominated international discussion about development and international assistance to Africa. According to this debate, the problem of persistent underdevelopment in sub-Saharan Africa is mainly due to a poor governance environment. A World Bank study in 1989 stated: 'Underlying the litany of Africa's development problems is a crisis of governance' (World Bank 1989: 60).

Governance can be understood in terms of three major components. First, it denotes the form of political authority that exists in a country: parliamentary or presidential; civilian or military; autocratic or democratic. Second, the means through which authority is exercised in the management of economic and social resources. Third, the ability of governments to discharge government functions effectively, efficiently and equitably through the design, formulation and implementation of sound policies and programmes. In short, governance refers to the exercise of political, economic and administrative authority to manage the affairs of a nation. Governance embraces all the methods — good or bad — that societies use to distribute power and manage public resources and problems. 'Good' or 'sound' governance is therefore a normative concept and a subset of governance that refers to governance norms (Leftwich 1993; UNDP 1995, 1997).

Good governance is regarded as a prerequisite for sustainable growth and development for a number of reasons. First, good governance is related to the necessity to create extra-economic conditions, important for the growth of African economies; for example, an effective public administration, a functioning legal framework, efficient regulatory structures and transparent systems for financial and legal accountability. In this context, the issue that makes good governance such an important prerequisite to growth and development is the quality of public goods supplied at country level.

The concept of good governance refers to the developmental potentials of democratic challenge. Accountability, rule of law, freedom of expression and association, and public choice of government are important elements of Africa's renewal. Good governance also refers to the consolidation of market reforms, although quite different development paths may be possible within the context of market-oriented economic systems. Good governance therefore requires the adaptation and continuous improvement of market-oriented systems in a specific socio-economic context (Bratton and Hyden 1992).

In short, the nexus between good governance and sustainable growth and development lies in the claim of good governance to support market-oriented socio-economic systems, provide adequate public goods and the possibility of public choice in a democratic environment (Turner and Hulme 1997).

Good governance, it is argued, creates a conducive environment for the implementation of structural adjustment programmes. Experiences of adjustment confronted international institutions and bilateral donors with the reality of incompetent and often corrupt governments in many developing countries. This was especially true in sub-Saharan Africa, and led to the World Bank identifying poor governance as a major source of the African crisis in its major report on the continent in 1989 (World Bank 1989).

The task of good governance as a facilitator of structural adjustment is to strengthen the fiscal integrity of the state, the enhancement of the state, the state's capacity for policy formulation, implementation and analysis; and the competent monitoring of the working of a liberalised economy. Improved governance does not therefore require some minimal mechanical reduction of the role of the state; but rather a redefinition of its role and ways it responds to the requirements of sound economic management. Indeed, the experience of most African countries suggests that the market economy requires for its success the assumption by the state of new 'tasks', especially in the areas of fiscal and monetary policy, and effective supervision of banking and non-banking institutions, as well as burgeoning capital markets (Brautigam 1996).

The Idea of the Developmental State

The relative success story of the new industrialising Asian countries such as Singapore and South Korea is often associated with the practice of the idea developmental state, which emphasises the creation of an efficient governmental bureaucracy, relatively autonomous of particular groups, and, more especially, of particular sections of the indigenous bourgeoisie; the development of a politically insulated, technocratic elite of economic policy-formulators; restraints on trade union activity; and the development of techniques of encouraging public saving.

Emphasis on the determination of the elite and relative state autonomy has helped to shape very powerful, highly competent and insulated economic bureaucracies with authority in directing and managing economic and social development. Leftwich (1993) has pointed out that what differentiates South Korea's Economic Planning Board and the considerable 'policy autonomy' of the Economic Development Board in Singapore, regarded as economic high commands from the generality of planning institutions in so many African countries, is their real power, authority, technical competence and insulation in shaping development policy. Their existence, form and function, need to be understood, once again, as consequences of politically driven urgency for development, and the politics of the strong state; and not as attributes of the principles of good governance. Indeed, the idea of an authoritative economic bureaucracy shaping the goals and strategy of development policy fundamentally contradicts the contemporary theory of, and prescription for, good governance. Whether democratic or not, developmental states have not been pleasant states by either liberal or socialist standards. They have frowned on dissent, and handed out rough and sometimes brutal treatment to student, labour, political and religious organisations, which have opposed them; and used a variety of internal security measures to suppress, banish or eliminate opposition.

In addition, two administration and governance strategies have emerged in Africa since independence, which have run counter to the ideals of the Asian developmental state: political and personal concerns of leaders, and neopatrimonialism. These strategies have caused African leaders to pursue short-term destructive policies and programmes, which have not promoted development, not least in the economic sector (van de Walle 2003).

Unlike Asian state elites of the same period, perceived as having been strongly oriented towards developmental goals, African post-independence elites appear to have been motivated more by political and personal concerns than by economic and social development. After independence, African leaders were concerned with the twin objectives of staying in power and building an economic base for themselves.

Apart from authoritarianism, an important, non-coercive from of consolidating power has been reliance on patronage. Resources needed for effective, broad-scale development were drained away. Their reasons included supporting regime efforts to consolidate power. To secure political incumbency, public benefits have been distributed and opportunities provided along political lines. Thus in their quest for self-preservation, state elites have dispensed government-controlled resources — jobs, licenses, contracts, credit — to select political allies as well as mediating access to economic opportunities in favour of close associates so as to enhance their hold over state power. In Africa, ethnic identities have comprised key bases for building clientelistic coalitions. Political leaders have allocated public resources and amenities to key intermediaries and their ethnic clienteles in ways designed to fashion a following and ensure political support. As a result, most regimes have been identified with specific ethnic and regional interests. But many have also been able to consolidate their hold on state power for long periods by promoting a relatively ethnically balanced distribution of the resources of government (van de Walle 2003; Tangri 1999; and Bratton and Hyden 1992).

New Public Management

This approach, discussed in detail in the subsequent chapter, emphasises: the centrality of the citizen or customer; accountability for results; decentralised authority and control; market orientation of cost recovery; competition between public and private agencies for service delivery contracts; and the creation of semi-autonomous agencies for service delivery (Hood 1991, 1995; Manning 2001; Larbi 1999; Walsh 1995).

Batley (1997), in his five-year review of the 'changing role of government in adjusting economies', has concluded that the effect of new public management (NPM) on most African countries has been at best mixed. There have been some improvements in efficiency and mixed effects on equity. On the downside, in relation to the move to autonomise service delivery agencies, transaction costs of radical reforms tend to outweigh the efficiency gains of unbundling. Reforms that pursue the separation of purchasers from providers may have decreased accountability. Consequently, inequity has grown (Manning 2001; Batley 1997).

Contextual Variables Affecting State Capacity

Literature on this subject is very sparse, unlike earlier approaches, which considered state capacity building from narrow organisational and public management perspectives. The works of Englebert (2000), Levy and Kpundeh (2004), Crook (2004) have focused on the political and institutional contexts or realities within which public organisations operate. Levy (2004), for instance, has identified four propositions that take into consideration the political and institutional dynamics affecting building state capacity.

Political and Institutional Realities of Building State Capacity

Political 'principals' set the agenda for their 'agents', public bureaucracies, to implement. Consequently, the behaviour of public bureaucracies cannot be understood without attention to their politically derived objectives, while their capacities cannot be effectively built in isolation from broader systemic changes.

Pressure for performance on public officials can be strengthened through improvements in systems of horizontal, downward and outward accountability, using mechanisms such as hierarchical control structures, monitoring of bureaucratic behaviour by elected political leaders, electoral feedback to politicians and citizen users, evaluating the performance of service providers.

Country-specific realities, unlike the current 'undifferentiated, best practice, cooker-cutter approach', must be taken into consideration in efforts to build state capacity because political institutions and the structure of political interests underpin systems of accountability. Owing that public administrations are embedded in a complex and interdependent system, change processes are cumulative as change in any one part of the system potentially induces change in other parts (Levy 2004: 25-6).

Conclusion

Since the introduction of structural adjustment in Africa in the 1980s, there have been efforts to reform the continent's ineffective public sector through various state capacity building strategies. The results so far have been disappointing. The main reason for the failure is because reforms focused mainly on technocratic and managerial fixes, without paying adequate attention to the politics of building state capacity: the political and institutional realities affecting the reforms.

Even though the level of ambition of the reforms is very high, politics have tended to permeate the way in which the public sector operates, therefore making it more complex and difficult. A reasonable way out would be to address the political and institutional dynamics, and eliminate the clientelistic tendencies that have permeated African governments. This would mean blending three models of public administration operating in Africa: neo-patrimonialism, the classical model of administration, and new public management, which in the end may be a tall order.

The modernisation of the state in Africa involves measures to improve its capacity to perform its functions effectively and efficiently. It also involves a reduced role for the state, and facilitating an enabling environment for development. Specifically, it involves the state shifting its own expenditure away from consumption towards investment; refocusing its attention on core public functions — macroeconomic stability, law and order; liberalisation; deregulation; and providing strategic social services. In summary, this has been called the 'dynamics of state retrenchment' (van de Walle 2003).

Lessons from Africa's Past Experience of Building State Capacity

Firstly, building state capacity is an expensive venture. Consequently, for purposes of sustainability, short-term reliance on grants and loans from bilateral and multilateral organisations must give way to domestically generated revenues.

Secondly, reforms aimed at building state capacity in the SAP period were much more complex and difficult than in the immediate post-independence period, where the private sector was weak in influence, and politics tended to permeate the way the public service operates.

Implementing NPM measures in Africa may have contributed to the realisation that market-inspired reforms of government 'failures' do not work very well in conditions where the state remains weak and subject to informal influences. NPM has not succeeded in eliminating the clientelistic tendencies that tend to permeate African governments. In such a context, the creation of independent agencies is a step in the right direction. But owing to the manner in which NPM has been introduced as a 'technocratic' fix, its full effectiveness cannot be achieved.

African public services have been subjected to the influence of at least three models. In addition to NPM, it is clear that the principles of the classical model of public administration and the more informal practices associated with neo-patrimonialism — the notion organisations are principally run at personal discretion with little or no regard for formal rules — continue to be important (Table 1). The way in which African public services operate reflects cross-cutting influences from all three models. Therefore, implementing the objectives of NPM is continuous uphill task.

Capacity building is one side of the equation. The other side is capacity retention and utilisation. The central problem of capacity is that most African countries have not been able to retain high quality human resource capacities — they have lost them, at a time when rich Western countries are rediscovering the need to focus more seriously on developing leadership in the public services.

32

How to attract, retain and effectively utilise leaders at all three levels: strategic, team and technical, requires work on both the supply side, through capacity building interventions, as well as on the demand side, especially around the issue of incentives and policy prioritisation. Such considerations have led most industrialised countries to revisit their immigration policies – to enable them attract talent. It is not a coincidence that the loss of critical skills constitutes one of the most serious challenges confronting poor countries in recent years.

Both monetary and non-monetary incentives are crucial. Monetary incentives involve remuneration and performance management systems that are competitive, and at least comparable with what obtains in the private sector. This could prove impossible in the absence of effective accountability systems – political, managerial and technical – to ensure that every key actor is not only responsible, but also accountable, for the use and misuse of public resources, the ingredients of a positive organisational culture. Moreover, paying competitive salaries – especially to managerial groups – in certain circumstances, may help to jump-start sluggish economies and have implications for wider political processes.

Table 1: Three models of public administration operating in Africa

Dimension	Neo-Patrimonialism	Classical Model of Administration	New Public Management
Organisational Objective	Maintenance	Law and order	Development of power
Service rationale	Ruler	Rule	Result
Organisational rule	Patriarchal	Hierarchical	Disaggregated
Operational mode	Discretionary	Mechanistic	Decentralised
Staff orientation	Upward	Inward	Outward
Career	Favouritist	Fixed and closed	Flexible and open
Handling failures	Blaming others	Denying responsibilities	Learning lesson

Sources: Adamolekun 1999; Hyden 1983; Bratton and Hyden 1992; World Bank 1997; Larbi 1999; Turner and Hulme 1997; Lane 1993.

Chapter 3

Theoretical Drivers of Public Sector Reform Initiatives in Africa

Introduction

A number of theories have emerged which, in one way or another, influenced most of the initiatives implemented under public sector reform in Africa. These include New Institutional Economics (NIE), public choice theory, development theory and New Public Management (NPM). The tenets, advantages and weaknesses of these theories, and their relevance to public sector management in Africa, are discussed below.[1]

New Institutional Economics

New Institutional Economics (NIE), or neo-institutional economics, or new economic theory of the state, is based on the assumption that various strands in modern economics prefigure the development of a theory of institutions that is highly relevant to the interpretation of the public sector (Williamson 1986; Hodgson 1988; Eggertson 1990; Stiglitz 1987). The theory argues that political institutions may be chosen rationally by means of deliberation about appropriate rules for the patterns of interaction in society. Instead of taking institutions as given, NIE attempts to endogenise what has traditionally been regarded as exogenous (Lane 1993: Weiner and Vining 1996). NIE involves two theories: 'Agency Theory' and 'Transaction Cost Theory'.

Agency Theory

This theory formalises assumptions about the distribution of property rights and information in written contracts that define organisations. Organisations can be viewed as collections of explicit and implicit contracts, typically covering periods of longer duration than single transactions, and generally characterised by the incomplete specification of contingencies. Agency theory deals with the design of these contracts. In particular, it focuses on the relationship between principals and agents who exercise authority on their behalf. Whenever human interaction involves considerable transaction costs, due to the inter-temporal nature of the interaction, as well as to the complexity of the agreement involved, principal-agent problems arise (Stiglitz 1987).

The principal-agent relationship is constitutive of state institutions, in particular public policy making in democracy. Public policy, or the making and implementation of policies in the public sector, involves the problems of typical principal-agent relationships within the private sector (Lane 1993). The policy process and implementation stages typically involve attempts of the population as the principal to monitor the efforts of politicians and bureaux as the agents to live up to the terms of the contract agreed upon.

Principal-agent theory argues that principals must solve two basic tasks in choosing their agents. Principals must select the best agents, whether employees or contractors (or, for that matter, other third parties who serve as agents), and create inducements for them to behave as desired. Principals must also monitor the behaviours of their agents to ensure that they are performing their tasks well. There are, however, two problems facing the principal in choosing his agent. First, the principal can never know everything about an agent. A supervisor can examine a potential employee's education, skills, personality and background; but can never be sure of selecting the best person for the job. Potential employees will know more about their own qualifications than potential employers can ever learn. As a result, employers tend to hire lower quality applicants than desired. This is called the 'adverse selection' problem. Second, the principal can never be sure of knowing the full details of the agent's performance (Arrow 1985). There are always signals about an employee's performance, such as reports, complaints and direct observation, but the employer can never know the full story. Principals are thus typically at an informational disadvantage with respect to their agents; and agents therefore have an incentive to work to less than their capacity, since they know that performance inadequacies may not be detected. This is referred to as the problem of 'moral hazard'. Put together, the two problems explain the difficulties of managers controlling organisations (White 1985).

Relevance to Public Sector Reform in Africa

The principal-agent theory has a number of advantages. First, it is a method for dealing with transaction costs arising in collective action. Consequently, the theoretical emphasis, where the outcome of the activities of the agent depends on the effort of the agent and an unobservable random variable, permits analysis of a number of policy problems within an integrated framework, such as institutional choice (Lane 1993; Weiner and Vining 1996).

Second, public activities by means of the state result in a double principal-agent relationship in a democracy. On the one hand, there is the relationship between the population as the principal, and its agents in their capacity of rulers of the population. On the other hand, rulers may wish to employ staff to be active in the implementation of the wishes of the rulers, which entails that the latter become the principal of the former. The double principal-agent relationship between the electorate, government and administration is more relevant than the distinction between politics and administration (Lane 1993).

The relevance of the principal-agent theory, however, does not explain several important administrative issues for a number of reasons. First, while the market approach produces interesting insights, market metaphors in the public sector often produce distortions, because 'markets' themselves have imperfections. On the supply side, government often has relatively few choices in purchasing services. From the maintenance of law and order, to the provision of basic amenities, government can rarely call on more than a few suppliers. These suppliers enjoy a near monopoly status in the market; and as purchaser, the government must solve all of the problems that exist in monopoly markets. Even in such mundane services as the collection of garbage, the number of potential contractors is often deceptively small (Lynn 1987; Ayee 1994).

Second, the market is further distorted on the demand side because, for some items, government is often the only purchaser. For instance, farmers in Ghana are not allowed to sell cocoa, the mainstay of the economy, to anyone but the government. The so-called strategic sectors of the economy in most African countries such as water, electricity, mining and acquiring arms and ammunition are central government monopolies.

Third, the principal-agent theory does not adequately recognise the role that power plays in organisational — or, more broadly, in political — life (Perrow 1986: 230-1). Because it is based on market behaviour, it assumes relationships among equals with principals and agents each seeking to develop acceptable exchange. It thus neglects what Parsons (1960: 41) calls 'the central phenomenon of organizations'. It also neglects the considerable complexity in the environmental of agencies and the many cross-cutting political pressures on administrators. Mathematical models could theoretically capture these additional complexities, but it is unrealistic to think that the full range of power relationships facing public administrators could be modelled in equations (Ayee 1994).

Organisational goals are far more dynamic and evolutionary than the relatively static principal-agent model tends to capture (March and Olsen 1989: 66). Member of the legislature, for instance, may frequently change their minds about which goals administrators should emphasise; and administrators themselves must set priorities among the often evolve in collaboration between principals and agents.

Decentralisation policies, for example, are frequently modified as governments and organisations learn more about what works and what does not. In intergovernmental grant programmes, also, it is difficult to recognise who is the principal and who is the agent. Different levels of government take different responsibilities for different pieces of the same programme. The relationship here is more one of exchange than of constitutional collaboration. While dynamic goals are theoretically possible in the model, they move far beyond the static principal-agent theory and enter into a realm of enormous complexity (Ayee 1994).

Finally, the principal-agent structure of the state is characterised by ambiguity, opportunistic behaviour, moral hazard and adverse selection. The fact that democratic state institutions rest upon a principal-agent structure prohibits in no way the agent from reversing the relationship and regarding itself as the principal. No benevolent assumptions need be made about the conduct of state activities. The possibility of reversing the principal-agent structure of the state, having the population serve the interests of the state, makes it all the more urgent that institutional mechanisms to be found that limit the range of opportunistic behaviour, the dangers of moral hazard and adverse selection. However, there are transaction costs involved in restricting the degrees of freedom of the agent. Within any institutional setting, there are bound to be serious ambiguities about the rewards given to the agent, the desired actions to be taken by the agent and the causal link between actions and outcomes, as well as about the actual state of the public policy environment (Lane 1993).

Transaction Theory

Williamson (1985) has pointed out that, as with agency theory, the focus of transaction cost theory is the contract. But unlike agency theory, which usually treats agents as simply reacting to contracts designed by principals, transaction cost theory views the parties attempting to engage in exchange (transaction) as contracting both the terms of the exchange and their execution. The theory focuses on the role of the state in defining the basics of contractual arrangements, which depend on existing technologies and natural endowments. As technologies or endowments change, a process is initiated toward new contracts in which the state may play a profound role in minimising transaction costs by institutional innovation.

The prevailing structure of interests does not only enter public institutions as the building blocks of public decision making and implementation. Interests also affect the derivation of public institutions prior to on-going policy making. Institutional arrangements in the public sector may constitute so-called structure-induced equilibria, which may be changed rationally, contrary to what the sociological version of institutionalism implies (Lane 1993).

The contracting process is costly. It includes the structuring, monitoring, bonding, and residual loss costs of agency theory, and also the costs of negotiation. At one level, transaction cost theory considers the nature of specific types of transactions. At a broader level, it is concerned with which institutional arrangements best facilitate and economise which kinds of transactions (Williamson 1985; Weimer and Vining 1993).

Three important problems contribute to the costs of contracting. Firstly, a 'cooperation problem' arising when a contract could offer all parties a gain relative to the absence of a contract. To achieve a mutually beneficial contract, however, the parties must expend transaction resources that include the prerequisites for negotiating and enforcing contracts. Secondly, there is a 'division problem', which arises when different, mutually beneficial contracts offer different relative gains. Thirdly, there is a 'defection problem', which arises when non-compliance is in the self-interest of any of the parties (Heckathorn and Maser 1987).

Weimer and Vining (1993) have pointed out that transactions involving investments by one or more of the parties in specific assets, such as specialised equipment or knowledge, have much lower value in uses other than as part of the transaction. Parties who invest in specific assets are especially vulnerable to threats of compliance. Therefore, they may be unwilling to enter into contracts, unless they receive credible commitments that other parties will not behave opportunistically in exploiting their vulnerability. One of the central questions of political economy is how governments can make credible commitments to convince people that their investments will not be appropriated, and that the money supply will not be debased (Blackburn and Christensen 1989).

Relevance of Transaction Theory to Public Sector Reform in Africa

The concept of transaction costs is not clear. It remains a kind of residual: all the expenses made in order to reach a contract, whether personal or social. Could the reduction in transaction costs be measured by moving from a system of individual contracts to a hierarchy, such as the firm or the bureau? What should be included when it is said government has minimised transaction costs by reforming an institution as property rights or local government structure? (Lane 1993).

Public Choice Theory

Public choice theory is a strong variant of rational choice theory. The theory is concerned with the provision of so-called public goods that are delivered by government rather than the market, because, as with clean air, their benefit cannot be withheld from individuals who choose not to contribute to their provision. It assumes that political society is composed of self-interested individuals who coalesce around organised interests. Per force, interest groups, which tend to form around relatively narrow issues of special importance to their members, are created by individuals seeking specific, self-interested goals. Individuals join with other self-seeking individuals to acquire access to public resources (Grindle and Thomas 1991). The self-interest maximisation hypothesis is at the heart of the public choice theory.

The following principles underline public choice theory: public sector actors or officials behave as if they maximise their own interests; all social entities are fundamentally sets of individual actors; political interaction is based on voluntary exchange; politics as voluntary exchange requires the making of an economic constitution to guide the relationship between the state and the individual; and citizens provide rulers or the state with resources and power for which they expect a return of goods and services, as well as laws regulating society in return for what they are giving up (Buchanan et al. 1978; Buchanan 1987; Lane 1993).

Relevance of Public Choice Theory to Public Sector Reform in Africa

The public choice model is important for a number of reasons. First, it offers a coherent explanation for seemingly non-rational decision-making by governments. Why should governments adopt public policies and programmes that are harmful to society? The solution to the problem is to closely limit the activities falling under the regulatory power of the state. Second, it explains why 'the public interest' is not achieved. Third, by focusing on the power of vested interests, it demonstrates the barriers to reform that are created by pre-existing policies, and by the political relationships that they engender. In so doing, it explains why existing public policy is the result of an inevitable rationality of rent-seeking (Lane 1993; Grindle and Thomas 1991). It provides an explanation for the willingness of public officials to respond to the pressures and imprecations of lobby groups and other types of special interests. It also provides an explanation for policy choices that are detrimental to society as a whole in both the short and longer term, and offers a way of understanding the constraints on policy change that develop over time.

Despite its relevance, it is limited in being less able to explain how policy changes or policy itself can lead to broadly beneficial outcomes. It allows little room for public officials who adhere to particular ideologies, whose professional training provides them with independent judgment in the analysis of policy issues, or who may adopt goals that transcend the interests of any particular group or coalition. Instead, policy elites are creatures of vested societal interests, however, much they seek to work these to their individual rent-seeking advantage; and their actions – devoid of ideological or technical content – can be explained by motivations to maximise political support.

Public choice theory is unable to explain how, why, or when reform occurs, except through events or the appearance of wise statesmen or technocrats who, for unexplained reasons, exhibit behaviour that is politically irrational. Though it indicates the importance of the power-seeking motivations of decision makers, it tells us little about how their motivations are developed or altered over time (Grindle and Thomas 1991; Lane 1993; Turner and Hulme 1997).

Development Theory

Development is regarded as a multi-dimensional process that seeks to reduce poverty and inequality, expands the real freedoms that people enjoy, accelerates economic growth, and renews social structures, popular attitudes and national institutions (Todaro 2000; Bryant and White 1982). Indeed, a central plank of development is to overcome problems such as the 'persistence of poverty and unfulfilled elementary needs, occurrence of famines and widespread hunger, violation of elementary political freedoms as well as of basic liberties, extensive neglect of the interests and agency of women, and worsening threats to the environment and to the sustainability of economic and social lives' (Sen 1999:xi).

Problems of development have confronted all African countries since independence. Consequently, various policy prescriptions have been propounded: the 'big push' into self-sustained economic growth; the Westernisation of social institutions and practices; the repudiation of Westernisation in pursuit of an 'endogenous model of change'; the mobilisation of national resources and energies around 'giant projects'; and, conversely, the glorification of the slogan 'small is beautiful' for a strategy based on small, locally controlled projects (Goulet 1992:467-75).

Aside from these policy prescriptions, a number of perspectives have emerged, including: the economic perspective of development; the dependency perspective; the basic needs perspective; and the development administration perspective.

The Modernisation or Economic Perspective

Development has been understood as an evolutionary process in which countries progressed through an identified series of stages to become modern. This perspective dominated development thinking in the period after the second world war. It became an almost integral part of the post-war orthodoxy in economic thinking that 'underdeveloped countries are held down very firmly by a circular constellation of forces to their low income equilibrium from which they can be jerked only be a concentrated large-scale development effort; by a big push of heroic dimensions' (Myint 1965:11).

The only strategy considered able to bring about this big push was a high rate of growth and industrialisation, leading to a high rate of growth in per capita income. This view was further refined by 'accounting concepts stemming from Harrod and Domar transformed development to a process of growth resting on a few quantifiable variables' (Currie 1978: 2). The idea of big push was further strengthened by Rostow's theory of stages of economic growth and the idea of 'take off' being closely linked with maximisation of the rate of growth (Rostow 1959).

Development as economic growth is measured by aggregative instruments such as product or income per capita, Gross National Product (GNP) and Gross Domestic Product (GNP); and is based on the assumption that the benefits of GNP and GDP will 'trickle down' to the less fortunate (Bryant and White 1982).

This view of development gained wide currency because it accorded not only with the popular notion of the underdeveloped country but also corroborated prevalent social science theories and formulations. In both cases, an underdeveloped society was defined as a 'closed traditional society, stagnating in primi-

41

tive isolation' (Myint 1965: 11). The prevalent dogma in sociology was the Parsonian variable approach, which characterised underdeveloped societies as ascriptive, particularistic and functionally diffuse. The process of economic development consisted in transforming this pattern of social behaviour into a pattern characterised by achievement, universalism and functional specificity (Parsons 1951). An underdeveloped society thus suffers from a lack of social and geographical mobility and division of labour. It emphasises status rather than achievement, and consequently leads to low productivity (Islam and Henault 1979).

Relevance of the Modernisation Perspective

By the late 1960s, scholars and development theorists, realised that the modernisation perspective, with its emphasis on economic growth, had failed, due to increased poverty, indebtedness, political repression, economic stagnation and inequality in African countries. The modernisation perspective is an oversimplified model of development that lacks two essential ingredients: an adequate historical input and a structural slant. Historically, it is ethnocentric, and ignores a wealth of evidence, which indicates that the process of economic growth cannot be encapsulated in simplistic notions about the displacement of traditional value systems and institutions by 'modern' ones. Structurally, the perspective is insensitive to the specific ways in which economic growth factors, such as the introduction of new technology or markets, may be interpreted, or modified or accommodated, within existing social relations. In addition, the inequalities of power and social class that structure these relationships are virtually ignored (Webster 1984).

The variant of the modernisation perspective that has come under attack is GNP per capita as an unreliable indicator for measuring development for three reasons. First, it consists of national averages, which, on their own, say nothing about the distribution of resources among the population. Second, it omits certain activities, such as work of domestic labourers, work of families in producing food for their own consumption, and the illegal and informal activity of the economy that occurs in every country in the form of corruption. Third, development cannot be measured in straightforward quantitative monetary terms. To understand development in bald terms of GNP is to ignore the way in which the value it represents is distributed among members of society. In short, GNP does not measure items that are important to welfare in most societies such as the distribution of income and wealth, employment status, job security and opportunities for advancement and availability of health and education services (Webster 1984).

In spite of its weaknesses, the modernisation perspective is relevant to African countries because it rightly focuses our attention on the role of values and attitudes in affecting people's behaviour, thereby their response to and fashioning of social change. Since the values and attitudes that people in Africa draw on do not necessarily express ambitions of 'achievement', they may well draw on 'traditional' values as repositories of some security and, at the same time, express values of 'nationalism' and perhaps 'self-reliance' as resources of social change (Webster 1984).

The Dependency Perspective

The dependency perspective originated in the 1960s through the work of a number of academics and development economists. They dismissed notions of the modernisation perspective that lack of development was attributable to a deficiency in appropriate modernising values; and that exposure to developed countries could only be of positive benefit to developing countries. Instead, they argued that massive and persistent poverty in developing countries was caused by exposure to economic and political influences of developed countries (Frank 1971; Rodney 1972; Amin 1972).

From the dependency perspective, underdevelopment is considered a process whereby colonialism arrested normal growth in the colonised countries of Africa. For example, the process transformed agriculture, which was a source of feeding people in these countries, to a subdivision of the agricultural system of the metropole. Thus, the colonies began producing cash crops — cocoa, cotton, rubber, peanuts, tea and palm oil, raw materials and consumption goods for the industrialised metropole, achieved by force, taxation, direct plantation, marketing boards and low prices (Rodney 1972).

From the dependency perspective, underdevelopment is a function of dependence. A widening gap between the centre — the US, Western Europe, Japan and the then Soviet Union — and peripheral developing countries was responsible for the crisis of development. Wage increases and apparent socio-economic stability could only be maintained at the centre at the expense of workers and peasants in periphery (Frank 1971). The problem of underdevelopment could therefore only be resolved through global redistribution of surplus, and fundamental change in the relations of production within the periphery itself (Cohen 1973).

The dependency view of development places great emphasis on external factors. Underdevelopment is a result of African society's dependence on the advanced countries. The phenomenon is replicated as internal colonisation with a dependent country. Dependence theorists believe that the impact of external factors is essentially negative, and growth at the periphery a function of expansion at the centre. Thus, economic growth is geared to the needs of the developed rather than developing countries. It is argued that international trade and finance frequently function to place developing countries at the mercy of factors beyond their control. Consequently, the importance of social and political structures in society is emphasised. International forces work to create 'structures of poverty' – institutions that respond to the priorities of the advanced countries– and in so doing, reinforce the poverty and dependence of developing countries (Frank 1971). The only way to stop the transfer of exploitation, and therefore promote development, is to break the chain of dependency through a working class revolution.

Relevance of the Dependency Perspective

The relevance of this perspective to public sector management can be seen in its political implications.

Dependency draws attention to the different interests at stake in African countries and the antagonisms between them. Growth benefits are not spread throughout the economy, as the modernisation theory would lead to believe. More importantly, there are conflicting interests in society: those with power use growth to promote their own interests. Terms of trade, choices about what to produce, and patterns of investment all strengthen the interests of certain groups in society at the expense of others. A nation is not simply a single national entity; it is composed of many, and often conflicting, interests (Hyden 1983; Leys 1975).

Dependency theory affords a different understanding of the potential oppressive role administrations can, and sometimes do, play. The inefficiency and arbitrariness prevailing in African bureaucracies sometimes reduce the poor to an increasingly marginal existence.

However, despite this relevance, the main weakness of the dependency perspective is that the concept of 'dependency' is much too vague to be of much use in the age of globalisation which emphasises interdependence; failing to clarify sufficiently ways in which African countries are dependent on developed countries. It is a circular argument: dependent countries lack capacity for autonomous growth because their structures are dependent ones (Webster 1984).

The Basic Needs Perspective

The new economic thinking to have emerged from dependency perspective, and as a result of the work of the World Bank-International Labour Organization (ILO), which appeared in the early 1970s, is an orientation to basic needs in development. This is turn demands a new international economic order. At the heart of this approach lies a desire for social justice and welfare based on the concern that the material resources of a society, including all assets or resources of the society: public goods (government funded services such as hospitals and schools), and capital for investment in agricultural and industrial enterprise, should be distributed more evenly throughout the population (Webster 1984). Development is thus defined in terms of the fulfilment of basic needs: hunger, malnutrition, health care, disease, clean water and shelter. It is an improved strategy than simply increasing income, because consumers are not always optimisers, and may not spend their income to meet basic needs.

The rural sector of the economy has become the major focus for basic needs based development through measures such as the direct provision of services for basic needs, indirect satisfaction through the creation of employment, development of agriculture which relies on a strategy of intensive labour, and decentralised planning with inputs from the grassroots (Islam and Henault 1979).

The focus of development envisioned by the basic needs perspective is reflected in Table 2.

Table 2: Basic needs perspective of development

Development has shifted from:		
Industrialisation	▶	Agriculture
Urbanisation	▶	Rural development
Market determined priorities	▶	Politically determined basic needs
GNP per capita	▶	Welfare of individual
Capital intensive	▶	Labour intensive
Top-down planning	▶	Participative-interactive planning
Foreign dependence	▶	Self-reliance
Advanced technology	▶	Appropriate or intermediate technology
Parallel development of sectors	▶	Integrated development of sectors
Economic orientation	▶	Socio-economic, political orientation
Service oriented rural development	▶	Production-welfare oriented rural development

Source: Islam and Henault 1979: 261.

Relevance of the Basic Needs Perspective

The perspective is a step towards balanced urban-rural development. It may discourage rural-urban migration, and in the long run, lead to increased production. The downside is that it is very expensive: cost constraints alone limit the speed with which policies can be implemented. Owing to acute financial problems facing governments in Africa, it many also be impractical on a large scale. Indeed, it has been observed that a country would cease to be underdeveloped as soon as it is in a position to provide all the available basic amenities to both urban and rural dwellers.

The Development Administration Perspective

Development Administration (DA) was coined in the mid-1960s. It was intended to play a major role in facilitating development. It resulted from the identification of administration as the primary obstacle to development, as opposed to economics (Stone 1965). DA may be seen as the practical application of the modernisation theory, and, the 'midwife for Western development – creating stable and orderly change' (Dwivedi 1994: 4-5). It is an American and European administrative tradition, rooted in scientific management, the experience of the US depression, the second world war, and ultimately, in the Marshall Plan for the reconstruction of Europe. It provided the background against which development engineering was conceived (Riggs 1970; Esman 1988).

DA focuses attention on the construction and improvement of a public administration system, as part of the total effort of national development. It covers both the administration of development: public administration as an instrument of national development, and the development of administration: measures to enhance the administrative capacity for development (United Nations 1975).

The key features of DA in its early period of existence can be summarised as (Turner and Hulme 1997:12-13):

- The notion of big government as the 'beneficent instrument of an expanding economy and an increasingly just society'.

- DA as synonymous with public administration, which was synonymous with bureaucracy; existence of an enlightened minority, such as politicians and planners committed to transforming their societies into replicas of the modern Western nation state.

- With an elitist bias.

46

● As tackling head on the lack of administrative capability for implementing plans and programmes through the transfer of administrative techniques to improve the central machinery of national government; foreign aid was the mechanism by which the missing tools of public administration would be transferred from the West to the developing countries.

● Culture was early recognised as an impediment to the smooth functioning of Western tools and dominant Weberian models of bureaucracy.

● Development administration had to overcome such cultural obstacles, regarded as sources of bureaucratic dysfunction.

However, by the late 1960s and early 1970s, these features of development administration were found to be unconducive to development. Indeed, the blame for poor developmental performance was in large part attributed to the failure of development administration (Turner and Hulme 1997: 13). In addition, scholars began to focus more closely on the environment in which administration was practised, the origins and maintenance of its ideological support, and alternative forms of organisational approach to development (Dwivedi and Nef 1982).

Development administration was in 'deadlock' (Schaffer 1969) and in 'crisis' (Dwivedi and Nef 1982). Reformulation of the features of DA into contemporary themes was called for. Some contemporary common themes of DA are: governments are limited in their capacity, and these limitations are incorporated into the design of public programmes; because governments 'cannot do it all', alternative and complementary channels need to be identified and fostered; programme designers recognise and capitalise on the pluralistic properties of public administration; participation is an important dimension in the administration of public services; societal contexts provide both specific opportunities and special constraints for development administration; there is enhanced appreciation of the uncertainties and contingencies inherent in deliberate efforts at developmental change; and, there are renewed pressures on government to extract greater productivity from continuing expenditures and reorient government bureaucracies to serve large disadvantaged publics more responsively (Esman 1988:125-34).

Relevance of the Development Administration Perspective

This perspective is relevant to public sector management in Africa in two ways. Firstly, in its premise that public administration is an indispensable instrument of economic and social development. Secondly, DA represents a realistic set of expectations about the process of development and the potentialities of the public sector in African countries. It allows for the study of issues such as privatisation, the efficacy of the market, popular participation and the role of non-governmental organisations. It emphasises the environment within which administration is practised, by focusing on both the relations between bureaucrats, politicians and organisations, and also power and politics (Turner and Hulme 1997: Riggs 1964; Swerdlow 1975).

New Public Management

The new public management (NPM) perspective is often associated with positive, action-oriented phrases such as: reinventing government, re-engineering, revitalisation of the public service, organisational transformation, total quality management, paradigm shift, entrepreneurship, empowerment, results-over-process, downsizing—and 'rightsizing', lean and mean, contracting out, offloading or outsourcing, steering rather than rowing, empowering rather than serving, and earning rather than spending (Frederickson 1996).

NPM captures most of the structural, organisational and managerial changes that took place in the public services in the Organization of Economic Cooperation and Development (OECD) countries such as the UK, and New Zealand and Australia in the late 1970s. It is a body of managerial thought or an ideological thought system based on ideas generated in the private sector, and imported into the public sector (Hood 1991, 1995). NPM shifts the emphasis from traditional public administration to public management, and pushes the state towards managerialism. The traditional model of organisation and delivery of public services, based on the principles of bureaucratic hierarchy, planning, centralisation, direct control and self-sufficiency, is replaced by a market-based public service management or 'enterprise culture' (Larbi 1999; Walsh 1995; Hood 1991).

Since the 1990s, the doctrinal components of NPM have evolved and been expanded. For example, the core ideas of the UK's 'citizens' charter' initiative, launched in 1991, added a consumerist dimension to public management. This charter brought the issue of consumers to prominence and has since become a key feature of most of NPM discussions (Hood 1991).

Key Components of New Public Management

Key components of the NPM may be divided into two strands. The first consists of ideas and themes that emphasise managerial improvement and organisational restructuring: managerialism in the public sector. These clusters of ideas tend to emphasise management devolution or decentralisation within public services. The second strand contains ideas and themes that emphasise markets and competition. In practice, these strands overlap. There is effectively a continuum ranging from managerialism at one end, for example, decentralisation and hands-on professional management, to marketisation and competition at the other, for example, contracting out (Gow and Dufour 2000; Walsh 1995; Larbi 1999).

The components or leading ideas of NPM can be summarised as (Gow and Dufour 2000: 573-97; Manning 2001: 297-312):

- A belief in the superiority of private sector approaches; development of stronger external orientation.

- Incorporation of foresight and anticipation into decision making.

- A shift from process-oriented to results-oriented government.

- The importance of visionary leadership at all levels and throughout organisations.

- The need to change the culture of the public sector.

- The development of alternative organisational designs based upon the principles of decentralisation, de-layering and openness to outside influences.

- The promotion of continuous organisational and individual learning, including the development of key competencies of employees.

- The widespread use of empowerment, teamwork and participation in decision-making.

- The development of a focus on the customer or client as the chief source of feedback on how well the organisation is doing; the need to manage diversity both within an organisation and in terms of the people it serves.

- The development of more robust performance measurement systems.

- The use of more imaginative types of incentives to promote improvements.

- Reshaping of the boundaries between the public and private sector through privatisation.

- Contracting out and partnerships.

- The demonstration of greater responsiveness to ministers, and greater accountability to legislatures and the public.

The shift from old public administration to new public management characteristically involves: re-working budgets to be transparent in accounting terms, with costs attributed to outputs not inputs, measured by quantitative performance indicators; viewing organisations as a chain of low-trust principal/agent relationships (rather than fiduciary or trustee-beneficiary ones), a network of contracts linking incentives to performance; disaggregating separable functions into quasi-contractual or quasi-market forms, particularly by introducing purchaser-provider distinctions, replacing previously unified functional planning-and-provision structures; opening up provider roles to competition between agencies or between pubic agencies, firms and not-for-profit bodies; and deconcentrating provider roles to the minimum feasible sized agency, allowing users more scope to 'exit' from provider to another, rather than relying on 'voice' options to influence how public service provisions affects them (Dunleavy and Hood 1994: 10). See also Table 3.

Table 3: New Public Management and its Core Measures

Variable	Managerialist Measures	Enabling Factors
Professional management	Delegating management authority within public services	Breaking up existing bureaucracies into separate agencies
Output control	Results orientation and funding of outputs, not inputs	Encouraging greater awareness by adopting 'citizens' charters'
Operational efficiency	Greater discipline and parsimony in resource use and fees for services rendered	Greater competition in the public sector
Terms of service	Flexibility in hiring and firing employees	Downsizing and public service and limit union influence
Budgeting	Make budgets more transparent in accounting terms	Encourage governments to become more enterprising by earning, not spending

Sources: Gow and Dufour 2000: 573-97; Dunleavy and Hood 1994: 10; Larbi 1999; Manning 2001: 297-312.

Relevance of NPM to Public Sector Management

The relevance of the NPM to public sector management can be found in the following main areas.

I. Decentralising Management, the Disaggregating and Downsizing of Public Services

The trend toward decentralised management in public services is part of an effort to 'de-bureaucratise' the public services and 'de-layer' hierarchies within them. Six dimensions of decentralising management may be identified (Dunleavy and Hood 1994; Hood 1995; Larbi 1999):

- Breaking up monolithic bureaucracies into agencies; for example, in Ghana and Uganda, customs and excise and internal revenue departments were hived-off from the civil service to form separate agencies in the 1980s.

- Devolving budgets and financial control, which takes the form of creating budget centres or spending units; giving managers increased control over budgets for which they are held responsible; this usually goes with the setting of explicit targets for decentralised units.

- Organisational unbundling, which involves the de-layering of vertically integrated organisations: traditional 'tall hierarchies' assume flatter and more responsive structures formed around specific processes such as paying of benefits.

- Downsizing: rationalisation and trimming the public sector in order to achieve 'leaner' (smaller or compact) and 'meaner' (more cost-effective) public services.

- The separation of production and provision of functions, which implies making a clearer distinction (organisational and financial) between defining the need for and paying for public services (indirect provider role), and actually producing those services (the direct provider role).

- The adoption of new forms of corporate governance and the board of directors' model, which entails the reduction of the power of elected representatives and minimising the influence of labour unions on management.

II. Performance Contracting

This has become an instrument of reforming state-owned enterprises (SOEs). Contracting out of the provision of public services is part the effort to reconfigure state-market relations, in order to give prominence to markets and the private sector. It involves legal agreement, be this for the supply of goods or the provision of services by other actors. Contracting may be between a public organisation and a private sector firm, or between one public organisation and another, as for example in the case of competitive tendering; or between management and an internal work force bidding to provide services in-house. The rationale for contracting out is to stimulate competition between service-providing agencies in the belief that competition will promote cost-saving, efficiency, flexibility and responsiveness in the delivery of services (Savas 1987, 1989).

III. Introduction of User Fees or Charges

The introduction of user fees or charges has been one of the major developments in the provision of public services under structural adjustment programmes (SAPs), when privatisation is not being pursued. Usually introduced as a condition for sectoral adjustment loans, they form part of the cost recovery measures and efforts to share the cost of publicly financed services with users (World Bank 1994). Charges to consumers for public utilities, such as water and electricity, have increased in African countries.

A number of institutional constraints and capacity issues have been identified in the application of NPM in African countries. Generally, capacity concerns include the ability to manage a network of contracts, the development of monitoring and reporting systems, and difficult governance and institutional environments constraining implementation capacity. With decentralising management, constraints include unreformed institutions such as centralised public service commission regulations and treasury expenditure controls, which prevent managers of decentralised units from having control over operational inputs. In general, there is reluctance in most central control agencies to devolve budgets and financial control, partly for fears around financial accountability, and partly because of the stringent regime of expenditure controls associated with the introduction of structural adjustment.

Main constraints of performance contracting include governments reneging on their commitments, and the assumption that an efficient market and private sector capacity exists to undertake the contracted out activities. (Larbi 1999; Gow and Dufour 2000; Manning 2001).

The Classical or Traditional Public Administration Model

The theories cited thus far are themselves influenced by two main approaches to public sector structuring: the classical or traditional public administration model; and the post-classical/traditional public administration model.

According to the classical public administration model, basic public administration principles according to which the public sector is or should be structured along the lines of institutional structure, the motivation of public employees and the status of the public interest are as follows.

The tasks of public institutions are to be decided by politicians but executed by administrators, in order to satisfy the model of rational decision making. Administration is based on written documents and this tends to make the office (bureau) the heart of modern government.

Public tasks are organised on a continuous, rule-governed basis. The rule according to which work is conducted may be either technical or legal. In both cases, trained individuals are necessary. Tasks and functions are divided into functionally distinct spheres, each furnished with the requisite authority and sanctions. Officers as well as tasks are arranged hierarchically, the rights of control and complaint being specified. All other things being equal, there is a preference for centralisation.

Resources of the organisation are quite distinct from those of the members as private individuals; and an officeholder cannot appropriate his or her office for private aims. Public employees are orientated towards tasks within the public sector in terms of vocation or a sense of duty to fulfil the obligations of their roles. In the public sector there is one dominating interest, the public interest, which sets limits to the influence of self-interests in politics and administration (Mill 1861; Wilson 1887; Weber 1978; Mintzberg 1983; Morgan 1986, 1990).

Three major criticisms have been levelled against classical public administration theory. First, that it is primarily a normative model for the conduct of the operations of the modern state, which may not necessarily be applicable to developing countries, which have different cultural, political and economic systems. Secondly, the model lacks descriptive accuracy. Thirdly, it fails to identify mechanisms conducive to the effectiveness and efficiency of the public sector; its capacity to explain how the public sector works is low (Lane 1993).

Post-Public Administration Models

Post-public administration models are oriented towards a post-Weber or post-Wilson conception of the public sector that attempts to develop new approaches to policy making institutions, implementation and management; features excluded by the classical public administration model. These models situate public institutions in liberal democracies more appropriately, since the principles of policy making, implementation and management bring in different theories of human motivation and efficiency or effectiveness in the public sector. The principles of the model are as follows.

The distinction between politics and administration is irrelevant and dubious (Appleby 1949). Rational decision-making is not feasible in public institutions; only bounded rationality is feasible (Simon 1947; Lindblom 1959; Wildavsky 1984). In the public sector, there may exist tendencies towards irrationality or a substantial risk of so-called garbage can processes (March and Olsen 1976).

Top-down policy implementation does not work. Therefore there cannot be automatic accomplishment of objectives in the public sector (Wildavsky, 1979; Pressman and Wildavsky 1984). Public administration is best handled by self-steering groups (Argyris 1960). Public administrators cannot be constrained by rules of procedure, as what matters is goal achievement and effectiveness (Novick 1965).

Centralisation in the public sector may be conducive to rigidity. Hierarchy in public administration could result in an implementation deficit (Crozier 1964; Hanf and Scharpf 1978). Systems of public institutions operate most efficiently when they are decentralised (Williams and Elmore 1976).

Public employees do not have a special type of motivation, but act in order to maximise self-interests such as income, prestige and power (Downs 1967; Tullock 1970).

Crucial to the discussion about the validity and applicability of the classical public administration model and other modern competing models is the concept of public interest. The public interest represents both the objectives and the institutions of making and implementing public decisions. Public sector spending, so it is argued in standard political science and public administration textbooks, is aimed at the accomplishment of the public interest. Proponents of the classical public administration model claim that the notion of the public interest notion is valid, either substantially, or in a procedural sense. They argue that the public interest will be forthcoming if the procedures of public institutions are correct; or when it is stated that the public interest is a specific objective to be pursued (Downs 1961; Lane 1993).

Conversely, implicit in public policy making (a post-traditional public administration model) is the implementation of public policy as a principal-agent problem. At the heart of the operation of public institutions is the notion that politicians, bureaucrats and professionals, as agents, are contracted to act in the interests of the citizens, as principals. According to this framework, the attempt by the principal to monitor the agent is critical. The challenge is to design a compensating system, through contracts, that makes the agents act, according to their self-interest, in the principals' interests? Typical principal-agent problems, such as behaviour opportunism, moral hazard and asymmetric information (Williamson 1986), plague the relationship between politicians on one hand and public employees of various kinds on the other (Lane 1993).

Amongst the new approaches to the modelling of the public sector, the public choice school questions the notion of public interest as the foundation for principal-agent relationships in the public sector (Buchanan 1986). New theories model the process of public sector expansion in rich countries as driven by fiscal illusions, egoistical behaviour on the part of special interests groups, and institutional failures in the public sector (Wildavsky 1985). Only mundane interests, self-interest and narrow collective interests exist in the public sector (Olson 1982).

Conclusion

This chapter has shown how the reform of African public services has been subjected to a number of theoretical influences. From the analysis, it is thus clear that all the theories point to three models of public administration actually operating in Africa. In addition to NPM, the principles of the classical model of public administration, as well as more informal practices associated with neo-patrimonialism: the notion that principal run organisations at their personal discretion with little or no regard for formal rules (as discussed in Chapter 2) continue to be important. The operation of African public services reflects cross-cutting influences from all these three models; and because of these influences, implementing the objectives of NPM is a continuous arduous task.

Chapter 4

Phases of Public Sector Reform in Africa

Introduction

Reforming the public sector in Africa is divided into three phases:[1] reforms from the 1980s to early 1990s, which focused mainly on macroeconomic stability and were mainly 'quantitative'; reforms of the mid-1990s to 2000, which focused on performance and civil service management; and reforms from 2000, which focused on service delivery as a result of the publication of the *World Development Report 1997*. See Table 4 for an overview of the aims, features, achievements and challenges of the phases.

Phase One Reforms: 1980s to Early 1990s

The phase one reforms of the 1980s to the early 1990s were 'quantitative' in outlook and focused on macroeconomic stability. Large scale, donor-funded civil service or public sector reform programmes only really began in Africa with the Structural Adjustment Programmes (SAPs) of the 1980s. Between independence and the late 1970s, the main focus had been Africanisation of the small inherited colonial civil services, combined with rapid expansion, particularly of education services. This process was aided by the former colonial powers mainly through training and technical assistance.

The SAP loans of the 1980s were primarily aimed at stabilising macro-economic crises of payment balances, fiscal deficits, runaway inflation and currency over-valuations. Civil service reform packages, which frequently accompanied SAP loans, were therefore mainly concerned with reducing the cost of public sector employment. This was regarded, self-evidently, as excessive or bloated, because it was unaffordable. The main problems of African civil services that had emerged during the economic crises leading up to structural adjustment are identified in Table 4.

Table 4: Phases of Public Sector Reform in Africa

Indicators	Phase 1	Phase 2	Phase 3
Period	1980s to early 1990s	Mid-1990s to 2000	2000 to date
Objectives	Achievement of macroeconomic stability	Performance and civil service management	Effective and efficient service delivery
Assumptions	Problems of service provision were the result of price distortion emanating from widespread government subsidies	Shifted emphasis from the quantity of employees to their quality. To make public sector employment more attractive and decrease the size of the government	(i) Improve service delivery to citizens, making it more responsive and effective; (ii) effective, responsive and legitimate state is crucial for sustaining marker economy
Features/strategies	Reducing size of state, cost-cutting, retrenchment, cost-recovery, privatisation	Features of NPM: remuneration and promotion policies to reward performance; incentives, skills, motivation, contracting out, public-private partnerships, agencification such as the executive authority model	Provision of basic services through processes driving pluralisation, decentralisation and participation; beneficiary surveys, self-appraisal exercises, performance improvement plans by public servants; customer-friendliness and responsiveness; Poverty Reduction Strategy Plans;
Achievements	Marginal reduction in size of public sector, even though it is debatable; cut back on equipment, services and development expenditure	Marginal improvement in conditions of service	Improved participation of civil society and other stakeholders in some public policies in the formulation of some public policies such as Poverty Reduction Strategy Plans; improved consultative process; marginal improvement in quality of service
Challenges/problems	(i) Ignored the historical evidence about the origin of the public sector problem in Africa. Low productivity and inefficiency originated from the economic crisis of the 1970s; (ii) reforms ignored a basic fact about people and organisations: people make organisations work, therefore, motivated workers are a sine qua non for organisational efficiency. It therefore failed to address livelihood concerns of public sector employees. (iii) lack of ownership of reform; (iv) real downsizing not achieved	(i) One-size-fits-all approach that ignores country-specific organisational aspects of public organisations; (ii) created a quagmire for employees, for instance, reduction in government requires that salaries and no-wage benefits remain low; due hiring freezes, the underpaid and poorly motivated workers were being admonished to assume additional responsibility and to lead efforts at improving efficiency. (iii) issue of relativities not addressed; (iv) brain drain continued; (v) lack of ownership	Performance improvement plans and beneficiary surveys have not been properly organised; provision of services for the poor still a far cry; in spite of participation, Poverty Reduction Strategy Plans have not achieved their objectives; quality of service not improved

57

It is estimated that in anglophone Africa, public sector wages declined 80 per cent in real terms between the early 1970s and the early 1980s, parallelling the general decline in GDP per capita income (van de Walle 2001: 134). For instance, in Ghana, in 1984, a top principal secretary earned only two and a half times the salary of a basic clerk, although, of course, there were substantial additional, non-pay benefits (Numberg 1996: 146).

During this period therefore, the now familiar problems of moonlighting, absenteeism, low morale, corruption and politicisation of recruitment emerged. There is little doubt that in many countries, the capacity of ministries, including finance ministries, to fulfil even the most basic tasks virtually collapsed.

Solutions offered by the 1980s civil service reform programmes were relatively crude. In line with neoliberal economic policies, aiming to drastically reducing the role of the state in the economy, they focused on: downsizing-retrenchments, mergers and recruitment freezes and eliminating ghost workers; and decompressing wage scales in an attempt to use savings on recruitment to pay higher salaries to higher level managers with scarce skills.

Large quantities of aid money were allocated for this purpose.1981-1991, the World Bank included civil service reform programmes as part of ninety-one loans or credit facilities worldwide. Fifty-five of these went to African countries, either through SAPs or Technical Assistance loans. They totalled US$2.13 billion (Numberg 1996: 122).

Phase Two Reforms: Mid-1990s to 2000

The phase two reforms of the mid-1990s to 2000 focused on performance and civil service management. The phase two reforms of the 1990s to some extent emerged from limited recognition that downsizing and pay restructuring alone were not producing the desired results. Net reductions in numbers were not great, except perhaps in the former SOE sector. Overall salary expenditure was actually rising. One authoritative World Bank study found that the idea that retrenchments and de-compressions would produce savings, which would fund real improvements in salary rates for skilled staff, had not worked (McCourt 1998; Dia 1996).

This phase retained the assumption that the civil service needed to be reduced in size. But it was accompanied with much more ambitious attempts to totally restructure the civil services, focusing on management systems, performance management and budget or financial management, as well as marketisation of service delivery.

As Richard Batley (1996) has shown about the changing role of government, this period of reform was nothing less than an attempt to transfer to African and other developing countries the techniques of public sector reform, which in the developed, particularly the English speaking countries, had come to be known as New Public Management.

The main problems of African public services before SAP have been summarised as follows (Hyden 1983: 145-7; Olowu 1999: 1-4):

- Norms about hiring and firing were rarely enforced.
- Resources tied for specific purposes were often diverted to meet urgent needs in other sectors.
- Attitudes towards both planning and scheduling were flexible and it was generally assumed that nothing occurs quite as arranged.
- Organisations tended to lack capacity for organisational intelligence, ability to learn from past mistakes is limited, decision-making techniques remain personal to the managers.
- Large-scale organisations tended to be divided into micro-organisations controlled by individual top managers.
- There was an erosion of real wage levels caused by massive inflation and the effects of import controls and compression of wage differentials.
- There was excessive expansion in the numbers of low level and poorly qualified employees, particularly in unproductive state owned enterprises and 'parastatal' agencies.
- Managers showed a marked ambivalence about technical matters.

The typical mechanisms for designing and implementing these reforms were the creation of high level reform agencies usually located in the presidential or prime ministerial offices, deliberately intended to by pass the mainstream ministries and backed up by teams of foreign consultants and technical assistance personnel. At the same time, foreign aid flows to African countries continued to increase massively, increasing the direct role of donors and their agents in government programmes especially public sector reform.

Phase Three Reforms: 2000 to Present

The phase three reforms following publication of the *World Development Report 1997* focused on service delivery. Phase three reforms only emerged since the end of the 1990s, following on from the World Bank's recognition that an effective, responsive and legitimate state was crucial for sustaining an effective market economy (World Bank 1997).

New generation programmes since the millennium, although still falling very much within the NPM paradigm, have tended to focus on the improvement, responsiveness and effectiveness of service delivery to citizens. They are normally specifically linked to the Poverty Reduction Strategy Plans, which have become a new conditionality for loans to Highly Indebted Poor Countries (HIPC), the majority of which are located in Africa.

Thus, for public servants, this has meant programmes which attempt to involve officers taking into consideration the opinions and demands of their clients — the public or users — and designing their own Performance Improvement Plans (PIPs), which involve service delivery standards monitored by both responsible managers and citizen user groups. The UK Department for International Development (DfID) is funding such programmes in, for example, Tanzania, Uganda and Ghana.

In fact, the Ghanaian Civil Service Performance Improvement Programme (CSPIP) started in 1996. This programme involved staff in targeted agencies engaging in 'self appraisal' exercises, in which they were supposed to confront and discuss public clients' feelings about the quality of their service; and come up with PIPs, which would then form the basis of a 'performance agreement' with their chief director and the government. PIPs should include measurable targets.

After twenty-four or more years the general consensus in both consultants' reports and in academic literature is that the results or achievements of the public service have been extremely limited. In some instances, they have even been negative.

Bureaucracy, Civil Service and Administrative Reforms

There is considerable disagreement over the record, primarily because reliable figures are hard to come by, even within individual countries. Comparative figures for creating aggregate results for the region or sub-regions are harder to come by still.

The World Bank review of 1999 concluded that on aggregate public sector reform programmes had been 'largely ineffective in achieving sustainable results'. Other analysts however argue that in selected important countries, civil service numbers fell in real term by up to about 10 per cent; and that by the mid-1990s, sub-Saharan Africa had the lowest ratio of civil servants to population of any group in the world: 1 per cent compared to 3 per cent for other developing countries (Goldsmith 2000; Olowu 2003: 113; Lienert 1998; Schiavo-Campo 1998).

In Uganda for instance, 1986-1996, the total fell from 239,000 to 159,000. In Tanzania, 1992-2000, it fell from 335,000 to 270,000 (Therkildsen 2001). Others argue that by the end of the 1990s, re-hiring (the revolving door syndrome) and redistribution cancelled out many of these reductions, for instance, in Ghana. They argue that a reduction in the civil service to population ratio simply reflects a decline relative to population growth (McCourt 1998).

As van de Walle (2001) calculates, African government expenditure on wages and salaries increased as a percentage of total expenditure. Expenditure on goods, services, transfers and capital expenditure decreased; even whilst overseas' aid increased from 5 per cent to over 10 per cent of GDP. The figures suggest that governments have attempted to maintain their core establishments and waged employees, whilst cutting back on equipment, services and development expenditure (van de Walle 2001: 96). It also seems likely that many skilled middle and senior officers left during the retrenchment phases (Olowu 2003:122).

Issues of Pay and Reward Systems

The record on increasing pay incentives tells a more depressing story still. From 1990-1996, real wage levels in most countries continued to fall on average by 2 per cent per annum (Lienert 1998); although in a few countries, such as Tanzania and Uganda, real increases were achieved: of 75 per cent in Tanzania, 1992-2000; and in Uganda nine-fold from a meaningless base. Only in Botswana, Africa's economic success story, have public sector wages kept pace with inflation, and at the same time, the total number of public sector employees increased in absolute terms by nearly four times, '24 Kwacha to 82 Kwacha', from the late 1970s to the mid-1990s (Goldsmith 2000:532). This is hardly surprising considering Botswana is one of the few African countries to have shown a significant increase in GNP per capita 1970-1998, which was six time higher, compared to an average fall of 9 per cent in other African countries.

Although much progress was made on de-compression, increasing differentials (Nunberg 1996:145), it failed to deal with the issue of relativities. Public sector salaries for skilled personnel became increasingly uncompetitive with the local private sector and the burgeoning NGO and donor agency sectors, which, by the end of the 1990s presented a far more attractive employment prospect for young African graduates.

For African professionals or managers with internationally marketable skills, the lure of emigration evidently became stronger; and the brain-drain, torrential. It is likely that around 60,000 middle level personnel emigrated from Africa from 1986 to 1990. The health sector remains especially vulnerable. In Ghana, it is estimated that a third of all trained health workers left the country in the decade 1993-2003. More two-thirds of trained doctors coming out of medical school left 1995-2002 (ISSER 2001). The number of Ghanaians emigrating to the US increased six-fold in the period 1986-1996 to comprise nearly everyone who had tertiary education or technical skills. The increased presence of expatriate technical assistance personnel on international salaries is a daily reminder to those who have remained of the enormous differentials.

For those on lower pay scales, a continuing problem in many countries has been the practice of non-payment for many months, as governments have sought to balance budgets.

Worst of all, most analysts agree that the primary objectives to improve the management of government budgets and programmes and capacity to offer better services have not been achieved. Even in the star countries such as Ghana and Uganda, which have received the largest shares of overseas development support over the past twenty years, budget tracking studies have shown that in Uganda, only 27 per cent and in Ghana 51 percent of budgeted grants for education actually reached schools. In the health sector in Ghana, only 32 per cent of central funds reached frontline services (van de Walle 2001:136). Revenue collection efforts have improved in some countries, for instance, through Ghana's Internal Revenue Service; but overall, the story is one of increasing reliance on donor aid and loans to support the larger parts of government and development budgets.

Training and Capacity Development

Serious training and capacity development problems beset the public service in most African countries, summarised as follows.

Training is often treated as a discrete event, not part of an overall programme of organisational development. Many trainees are selected on the basis of bureaucratic politics and patronage rather than on the basis of the greatest need. Competent trainers are rare, as training is itself a poorly developed profession. Training curricula and models are usually based on borrowed models that are rarely updated. Classroom-based, academic-style teaching dominates most training programmes, raising serious questions of relevance. Training evaluations are usually limited to assessing happiness levels rather than the impact on knowledge, attitudes, behaviours and job performance. Most training institutions are poorly financed and managed and are usually heavily dependent on government (Paul/World Bank 1983).

One of the initial tasks of civil service reform in Africa is typically the revision of the training policy, and development of a strategy document to reflect the new liberal and decentralised environment within which the civil service operates. The policy specifies the framework, including the purpose, opportunities, types and funding sources of the training, in order to ensure that all classes and levels of civil servants are covered, and that their training needs addressed. It also stresses the decentralisation of the training function, assigning full responsibility to the ministries, departments and agencies (MDAs) for the functional training of their staff (Olowu 1999, 2003).

Some of the training and capacity development strategies being adopted in the francophone countries such Senegal and Mali and the anglophone countries such as Ghana, Nigeria, Tanzania, Egypt and Uganda are shown in Table 5.

Table 5: Strategies of training and capacity development in francophone and anglophone African countries

i.   Job related training: While encouraging the acquisition of formal certificates through the granting of study leave with pay for graduate and post-graduate training, priority has since civil service reform been on improving skills to enhance service delivery. Emphasis has also been placed on short 2-3 day workshops and training sessions to reduce prolonged absence from work, associated with long residential training. Training in job related areas such as Policy Formulation and Analysis, Strategic Planning and Corporate Management, Target Setting and Performance Management, Improving Customer Care and Change Management.

ii. High flyer scheme: As an initiative aimed at building the capacity of the civil service and introducing new blood at the higher echelons, a high flyer scheme was introduced in some African countries like Ghana and Uganda. Under this scheme young officers who are deemed to have the potential are being given specialized training to enable them to maximize their potential and strengthen the capacity of the civil service through accelerated promotion if they are able to demonstrate their worth. For instance, in Ghana, as at 1998, 25 officers have been attached to private organisations such as Unilever, Mobil Ghana Limited, Social Security and National Insurance Trust (SSNIT) and Home Finance Company, to expose them to the way jobs are executed and programmes managed in the private sector. There is a further opportunity to sponsor officers who maintain high standards of performance to benefit from special training in both local and overseas institutions.

Table 5: Continued

iii. Revamping of training institutions: Governments in Egypt, Tanzania, Ghana, Uganda, Senegal have revamped training institutions and supplied them with electronic typewriters and computers. The curriculum of the institutions has also been revised to make room for the integration of computer programmes in the training of secretaries. In Ghana, for example, the Civil Service Training Centre in Accra and the Ghana Institute of Management and Public Administration (GIMPA) have expanded their activities to meet the increased demands of training as a result of the civil service reforms.

iv. Governments have requested Ministries/Departments/Agencies to include in their budgets substantial amounts for the training of their personnel.

vi. The training programmes have adopted a highly pragmatic approach to maximizing the effectiveness of all levels of staff. They have sought to ensure competency because they are increasingly tailored to individual needs.

vii. In line with the search to delegate more responsibilities to the Ministries/Departments/Agencies (MDAs), the Civil Service Councils (the policy making board of the civil service) in African countries have approved new guidelines to delegate authority for recruitment and promotions to individual service civil service organizations and thereby reduce the delays and frustrations in the former arrangements. The promotion processing period, which used to be about 1-3 years, has been reduced to 1-4 months. In addition, promotion is based primarily on merit and not on length of service. As the emphasis continues to shift from high security careers, shaped by length of service and seniority, towards shorter-term employment contracts and achievement-oriented promotion, a new cadre of responsive managers is emerging

viii. The generalist line for promotion is gradually being phased out.

ix. The introduction of open advertisements, people in the private sector/other public sector organisations which show interest could be appointed if found suitable. Open recruitment procedures, with wider recruitment for senior posts, help to ensure that vacancies are filled on the basis of skills and competence. As a result the assumption of a career-based civil service with semi-automatic promotion is weakening.

Sources: Ayee 2001a; Olowu 1999b: 1-23.

These strategies are aimed at professionalisation of the civil service. At senior levels, low reward, high security positions are replaced with the exact opposite. There is therefore a shift away from a career civil service to a service where appointments are mainly based on contracts, performance measurement and intra-service mobility. The expectation is that public sector managers, often recruited from the private sector, will have a high level of managerial skills and talent, and will be flexible enough to manage effectively in any government agency.

In spite of the strategies implemented to promote effective training and capacity development, problems are still experienced, because most of the training is not demand-driven and tailor-measured to actual jobs. In addition, training programmes are not continuous and compulsory at all levels. Most governments have been unenthusiastic about training because it involves a huge capital outlay, and is also not visible for the electorate to appreciate (UN/CAFRAD 1994).

E-Government

The promise of e-government, technology innovations to improving public-service efficiency, or technology innovations in the public service, has been well documented. The promises of e-government are summarised below.

E-government has the tendency to improve effectiveness, efficiency and productivity of government. For example, an integrated network-based national revenue management system will collect information speedily and effectively, enable revenue officers to receive cases more quickly and also automate and modernise the tax collection process.

The process of computerising government business is de facto a process of exploitation of government information resources. It is well known that one of the primary activities of government is record-keeping. As a result of computerization, government becomes the largest public information owner and manages vast resources of data.

E-government facilitates government information services. In democratic societies, one of the government's principal responsibilities is to report on its affairs to its citizens. The administration has the duty to inform individuals of their rights and obligations and to maintain good relations with them. An individual citizen's understanding of public service depends not only on its outcomes only, but also on the way in which he or she is informed.

By improving public access to information, e-government helps to foster transparency and accountability in government. E-government has spread the concept of a more efficient and responsive public sector, based on 'service management'.

E-government can change the modalities of public service delivery. For centuries, the notion that citizens might actively participate in all public affairs and make substantive inputs in policies remained a distant prospect. Currently, government websites, email and other means could turn such participation into a reality (UNDP 2001: 117).

E-government is regarded as the pursuit of a 'paperless' public service. As a result of its promise, it has been noted that administrative reform in African bureaucracies is increasingly dependent upon information technology (IT). Consequently, World Bank lending alone for IT has increased since 1981 by nearly 30 per cent per year, reaching US$570,000,000 by 1989 and US$745,000,000 by 2003 (World Bank 2003). Since the late 1980 and early 1990s, all African countries have embarked on establishing information technology and management information systems.

However, despite the potential for making government bureaucracies more effective, the performance of information technology-based reforms often falls short of expectations. In the public sector Africa, information systems fail or underperform more often than they succeed, because 'saints' (progressive government staff) are few; 'wizards' (technical assistance staff) are inappropriate, and demons (corrupt and apathetic officials) are many. The systems are complex and the organisations are weak (Peterson 1998:38-9). Information Communication Technology (ICT), which embodies systems development, is a personal and contingent process. It requires selling reforms to decision makers; establishing a learning relationship between users, designers and implementers; and building an effective design team, which African public services lack (Peterson 1998). Other factors that have militated against an effective ICT system in the public service in the public service in Africa are summarised below (Adamolekun 1999a: 116-7):

- There is little demand for information and little experience of the problems caused by ad hoc approach to information systems.

- There are insufficient in-house skills in strategic planning, information systems analysis, design and management, management services and project management. Requisite participation, openness, and feedback are absent.

- There is little willingness to share information between ministries and departments.

- The external environment is too unstable to permit long-term planning.

- There is a lack of in-house skills in numeracy, data presentation, and interpretation. Staff have unrealistic expectations and glamorise technology.

- Managers fear that computerisation will lead to a loss of control.

- Radical change is introduced without consultation.

- Funding for long-term maintenance of the computers, as well as for continuing management development, has not been secured.
- There is a lack of comprehensive policies on computerisation.

Outcome of the Reform Phases

Policy initiatives aimed at better equipping the public sector for the post-SAPs regulatory period have largely remained unsuccessful because they emphasise training, incentives, downsizing and institutional innovations, which Englebert (2000) has described as 'somewhat misguided'. In his words, which seem fatalistic:

> It is doubtful whether African bureaucrats need additional training and more imported institutions. They are neither less competent nor less moral than civil servants elsewhere. Patterns of bureaucratic inefficiency, corruption, delinquent rule of law, and the like answer to a political logic and are the consequences of the dichotomization between statehood and power in African non-legitimate states. It is hard to see how public sector management programmes address these deeper issues. They may provide temporary Band-Aids, but they are unlikely to bring about lasting improvements (Englebert 2000: 180-1).

In spite of the reforms, many public organisations have remained inefficient. Their continued poor performance has been blamed on a number of factors, set out below.

Reforms were mainly seen in technical and managerial terms rather than in political and institutional terms because 'public administrations are embedded in a complex, interdependent system. This system incorporates not only the bureaucratic apparatus as a whole, but also political institutions and social, economic, and political interests more broadly' (Levy 2004: 11).

Most of the reforms are nested in politics. For instance, whereas many governments agreed to reduce the number of ministries as part of the retrenchment exercise they have often resorted to the temptation of increasing the number of ministries again. The introduction of multi-party politics has reinforced the pressure to reward followers as part of coalition building in government. The result is that democratic reforms have often worked against the necessary consistency in reforming the public sector. The 'one-size-fits-all' approach ignores country-specific organisational aspects of public organisations (Lienert and Modi 1997; Nunberg 1996).

Reforms have failed to respond to the livelihood concerns of employees (poor working conditions and inadequate salaries for public sector employees have continued due to the need to reduce government expenditure) and requirement that recruitment be frozen with its attendant admonition to underpaid and poorly motivated workers to assume additional responsibility and to lead efforts at improving efficiency (Goldsmith 2000; Olowu 2003; Lienert 1998; Schiavo-Campo 1998).

African bureaucracies suffer from a weak organisational culture as a result of more emphasis being placed on motivation rather than on the public service ethos of commitment, professionalism and promoting public service and interest (Crook 2004).

There is low demand for quality service and good performance from citizens, clients, users and civil society organisations, which has made operations of public organisations not only unresponsive and unaccountable, but also fraught with neo-patrimonial logics (Crook 2004).

Conclusion

Trends in reforming the public sector in Africa show that they have been influenced by both economic liberalisation and democratisation. It is perceived that donors, rather than 'home-grown' forces have driven them. Each trend placed emphasis on accountability and improved service delivery. One significant outcome is that the reform trends show mixed results, mainly because public expectations of the state in Africa differ fundamentally, while the notions of public service ethos or civil service culture have not changed, as envisaged. Perhaps the legacy of the trends is to constrain public officials to ensure that public expectations provide a motive, and to build basic public sector disciplines to provide capability. Even though direct application of the reforms has been limited, and has achieved little in African states, they have significantly altered the public management debate both for governments and for development agencies (Manning 2001).

Taken together, the trends aimed at re-tooling public institutions to perform the regulatory functions, which the post-structural adjustment state was to perform. These reforms included: 'correct[ing] public sector institutional weaknesses' in Burkina Faso; 'establish[ing] a more favourable environment for private sector growth' in Chad; 'help[ing] the government to improve governance' in Madagascar; and 'build[ing]...capacity' in Tanzania. None of these were typically part of the 1980s SAP programmes (World Bank 1999:169-71). Additionally, the Bank has allocated increasing resources over the last few years to what it labels 'public sector management reform programmes'. Whereas adjustment lending represented about 13.2 per cent of the Bank's portfolio between 1990 and 1995, as against 3.3 per cent for public sector reform programmes, the ratios became 8.5 per cent and 6.8 per cent respectively (Englebert 2000).

Instead of making loans conditional on macroeconomic policies, public sector reform programmes actually finance improvements in bureaucratic services, the judicial system, and the overall provision of the rule of law. They typically consist in training bureaucrats or other civil servants, and shielding agencies from specific redistributive pressures, as was the case with the adoption of performance-based pay in the customs, excise and preventive service (CEPS) in Ghana (Dia 1996).

Based on the understanding that states fail to properly implement development policies and provide good governance of their economies, reform programmes attempt to better the African state, and to increase the effectiveness and efficiency of its institutions. From 2000, public sector management loans from the World Bank and IMF have included: support to Ghana's 'government efforts to improve the efficiency, effectiveness, and quality of public services'; and 'financing improvements in "capacity-building" in Mauritania'; and the 'efficiency of the public sector' in Niger (World Bank 1999:172-4). Similar loans have also covered the creation of a 'more secure legal and judicial environment for new investors and existing businesses' in Côte d'Ivoire; 'performance-based capacity building in Guinea' (World Bank 1998:130). They have sponsored the 'reform of public administration and the judiciary' in Madagascar, 'thereby increasing effectiveness, efficiency, and transparency in the public sector' (World Bank 1997a: 106). The reforms have emphasised training, incentives, downsizing and institutional innovations (Goldsmith 2000).

Chapter 5

Strategies of Public Sector Reform: The Balance Sheet

Introduction

Public sector reforms have been implemented in several African countries in several areas including in the civil service, judiciary and the tax system. They have included decentralisation, privatisation, deregulation, co-production and public-private partnerships. The outcomes of these strategies for the ability of the state to deliver have remained largely unsuccessful, limited and marginal (Tangri 1999; Olowu and Wunsch 2004, 1995; Rondinelli et al. 1989, 1996; Smith 1985; Mawhood 1993; Olowu and Smoke 1992; Wunsch 2000, 2001; Adamolekun 1999; Collin 2000; Olowu 1997; Englebert 2000; Dia 1996; Levy and Kpundeh 2004; Ayee 1994, 2001; Ayee and Crook 2003; Crook and Manor 1998; Devas, Delay and Hubbard 2001).

Some specific reforms are examined here, by way of selecting successful and unsuccessful cases, and explaining why some have succeeded while others have not. For reasons of space and a lack of information, it is difficult to examine all the reform efforts in the various areas. Reforms carried out in areas of state enterprise, decentralisation and the civil service have been selected because reforms have been carried out in these areas in most African countries. Therefore, useful and meaningful comparisons can be made.

State Enterprise Reforms

Evaluating the performance of SOEs has been complex and controversial because the main criterion of evaluating their performance – financial return – has itself generated much debate and controversy. The use of profitability or financial return poses a problem, as SOEs in Africa were frequently compelled to satisfy broader social ends. Examples are governments fixing the tariffs of SOEs at below existing market prices. SOEs have been created to pursue non-commercial goals. Their financial impact, for a variety of reasons, is not reflected in the accounts of SOEs. A more balanced way of measuring the performance of SOEs therefore is to consider both their financial and non-financial standing.

In financial terms, the performance of SOEs has been very disappointing. Net losses had been recorded by SOEs in all African countries, thus increasing the national debt. A few examples suffice. In Ghana, in 1982, the total operating deficit of SOEs amounted to over 3 per cent of GDP – equivalent to total government spending on health, education and social welfare.

In the early 1980s, in francophone African countries such as Togo and Niger, SOEs net deficits were roughly 4 per cent of GDP. Moreover, SOEs contributed little to government revenue; instead having constituted a major burden on government budgets. For instance, in Ghana between 1979 and 1983, the net flow of budgetary transfers to the SOE sector amounted to an average of about 10 per cent of total government expenditure (Appiah-Kubi 2001). Similarly, in 1989, subsidies to loss-making SOEs amounted to 14 per cent of the Zimbabwean budget (Grosh and Mukandala 1994).

Considered on non-commercial or non-financial terms, the performance of SOEs has been equally dismal. The provision of goods and services was below average. In practically in sectors such as agriculture, industries, utilities, insurance, banking, trading, manufacturing, air, land and sea transport business, SOE performances were inadequate, haphazard, unreliable, infrequent and unduly expensive.

In addition, limited results were also recorded in the multiple development objectives of SOEs such as employment generation, income distribution, regional equity, appropriate technologies, and export production (Bennell 1997; Nellis 1986; Tangri 1999; Ramanadham 1989).

In summary, SOEs have failed in the following ways. They were making heavy losses and were aptly referred to as waste pipes, so could only be kept by huge subventions from the governments. About half the total outstanding nonperforming assets of banking institutions was accounted for by the SOEs. Prices were generally set at levels which bore little relation to the real cost of production. The workforce in many establishments was bloated; appointments to executive grades were influenced not by ability and expertise, but by such considerations as political affiliation and nepotism. There has been an absence of effective private sector competition. The lack of a profit motive, induced a feeling of complacency in management. And decision making was almost paralysed by excessive bureaucracy and attitude towards state business (Ayee 1994b).

In short, SOEs in Africa have presented a depressing picture of inefficiency, losses, budgetary burdens, poor products and services and minimal accomplishment of their non-commercial objectives (Nellis 1986).

There is no doubt that governments in Africa viewed the public sector as the engine of socio-economic development. However, practitioners and theorists have agreed that reliance on the public sector has stretched the managerial abilities of governments beyond their limits. As attitudes have changed, and the burdens of present arrangements mounted, governments became increasingly aware that they must realign their priorities. Almost everywhere, governments in Africa became more inclined to mobilise skills and resources of the private sector in the larger task of development, concentrating government efforts on essential public services, pruning activities that have become unmanageable, and using resources more efficiently.

The Experience of Public Sector Reform: Privatisation, Commercialisation and Public Enterprise Liquidation Reconsidered

Privatisation and commercialisation are the most common types of reform of SOEs. The continuing interest of governments in Africa, and in other parts of the world, in the privatisation and commercialisation of state-owned enterprises (SOEs) has turned privatisation and commercialisation policies and programmes into important instruments for promoting market-oriented approaches to economic development. Privatisation and commercialisation have become integral parts of administrative reform in former centrally planned socialist economies, developing countries and post-industrial societies.

The UK and New Zealand embarked on major restructuring of the public enterprise sector in the beginning of the 1980s. In the UK, the emphasis of reform was on privatisation. In New Zealand, it was a combination of privatisation and commercialisation. Considered trailblazers, reform efforts of the public enterprise sector in both developed and developing countries have as a matter of course followed the approaches of the UK and New Zealand.

A combination of objectives was sought in the reform of SOEs in both developed and developing countries to: ensure profitability by avoiding trading losses; avoid liquidity crises and rising debts; restructure and rationalise the public sector in order to remove the dominance of unproductive investment; prevent state owned enterprises (SOEs) from being an ever-increasing burden on the government budget and to facilitate their access to capital markets; ensure positive returns on investments in restructured enterprises and improve the managerial and operational performance of those enterprises that will remain in the public sector; initiate the process of the gradual cession to private sector of the SOEs that, by the nature of their operations and other socio-economic factors, are best performed by the private sector; create a favourable investment climate for both local and foreign investors; provide institutional arrangements and operational guidelines that would ensure that the gains for the reform programme are sustained in the future; and encourage wider share ownership, especially among lower income groups (World Bank 1995a, 1995b; Rondinelli et al. 1989; Kikeri, Nellis and Shirley 1992; Lalaye 1999).

Defining Privatisation

The term privatisation is defined in various ways, connoting different things for different people. Part of the problem with discussing privatisation is that the meaning of the term is confusing; because it has been used to refer to several types of policy initiatives. These include the shift from public to private provision of goods and services, through contracting out or voucher arrangements, while maintaining public financing; the lessening of regulation from a shift of management rights from the public to the private sector; a shift in activity from one sector to the other; the disengagement or withdrawal of government from specific responsibilities under the assumption that private institutions — firms or voluntary organisations — will take care of them; and the sale of public assets (Hemming and Mansor 1988; Kolderie 1989; Butler 1985; Savas 1985; Shirley 1983; Shirley 1989; Moe 1987; Ramanadham 1989; Cowan 1990). The removal of controls on the private provision of goods or services — deregulation — is also sometimes described as privatisation. According to Young:

> ...privatization can be defined both in its narrow and broad meaning. In its narrow meaning, it simply entails a shift of productive activities or services being undertaken by the public sector to private ownership or control. In its broader meaning, it refers to a process by which the state's role within the economy is circumscribed while at the same time the scope for the operation of private capital is deliberately extended Young (1991:50).

The thread running through the differing definitions is the idea that inherent inefficiencies of government can be relieved by subjecting goods or services, traditionally provided by government, to the discipline of the marketplace. Competition among firms, freedom from red tape and other procedural constraints, flexibility in hiring, firing, and compensation practices, it is believed, create

73

pressures and opportunities for efficiency and cost savings that cannot be achieved in the public sector (Moe 1987; Savas 1985; Shirley 1989).

Two distinct and quite different objectives are pursued under the name of privatisation: the improvement of the delivery of goods or services by taking advantage of marketplace efficiencies; and, alternatively, the reduction or termination of public support for particular goods or services together, sometimes called load-shedding.

In the first case, privatisation does not eliminate government accountability for the results of its expenditure. It simply shifts the locus of service delivery. The means of policy implementation is privatised, but the functional sphere of government action is not. That which is relinquished 'may be the easiest part – the doing. The conceiving, planning, goal-setting, standard-setting, performance-monitoring, evaluating, and correcting all remain with the government' (Moe 1987: 23).

In the second case, government withdraws or reduces its role as a buyer, regulator, standard setter, or decision maker in particular service areas (Kolderie 1986: 288). According to some proponents, this is 'real' privatisation because it breaks up public spending coalitions and reduces the base of political support for government growth. Others argue conversely that this 'false' privatisation because for government to abandon a programme or responsibility is not to privatise it. For privatisation to occur, government must assure that something happens on the private side (Butler 1985).

In this book, privatisation, or divestiture, refers to the transfer of management and ownership of activities and assets from the public to the private sector entailing outright whole or part sale of assets, leasing, or utilising contract management. In short, in Africa, privatisation encompasses a diversity of contractual arrangements from outsourcing to lease or concession arrangements, to full divestment (Savas 1985; Shirley 1989; Tangri 1999; Caulfield 2006).

Forms of Privatisation

Six forms of privatisation may be identified.

Public Offer of Shares. Under this arrangement, the state-owned shares in the SOE are offered to the public at large, that is, replacing government ownership by public ownership.

Contracting out or Leasing or Private Placement of Shares. This involves the transfer of state-owned shares in the SOE to private individuals. It also enables the state to finance an SOE using a private firm to run it. Public works, urban development and water supply schemes are the most frequent users of this mode of privatisation.

Debt Equity Swap. The arrangement involves the transfer of ownership of an SOE to the private sector in settlement of its debt.

De-nationalisation or Liquidation. This form entails the break-up and/or sale of the assets of the SOE through a new share flotation on the stock market, or by closing down the SOE altogether. However, de-nationalisation may entail a transfer of monopoly from one inefficient owner to another, with no gain for the economy and its consumers, if certain measures such as restructuring, altering culture, adopting other forms of organisational change, and creating a competitive or regulatory environment that promotes efficiency, are not taken into account.

'Market Loosening' Strategy of Deregulation. This mode of privatisation involves what Turner and Hulme (1997) call the 'abolition of statutory barriers', which prevent private operators from competing with SOEs. For instance, monopolistic crop marketing boards have been abolished, or forced to compete with private companies. This would usually result in higher prices for farmers and increased output for the market. This changed environment makes it no longer worthwhile for farmers to engage in illegal trading across porous national borders to avoid the low prices of the crop marketing boards in their own countries. Governments may also use the deregulation to encourage private sector participation in infrastructure provision.

Self-management or Deferred Public Offers. This arrangement includes, for example, offering the shares of the SOE to its employees or workforce. In the agricultural sector, cooperatives or farmer associations may be used to take over the functions of the SOE. There may be problems of management capacity, or of management authority, in instituting reforms to make the enterprises more efficient. Lack of capital and inadequate back-up services are other reported problems (Kikeri, Nellis and Shirley 1992; Rasheed, Beyene and Otobo 1994; Ramanadham 1989; Butler 1985; Cowan 1990; Nellis and Kikeri 1989; Bienen and Waterbury 1989; Turner and Hulme 1997).

Defining Commercialisation

Commercialisation entails the reform of public enterprises so that their operations are subject to competition and market forces. There are two types of commercialisation: full and partial. Fully commercialised SOEs become entirely self-sufficient, with the capacity to make contributions to the treasury. They are supposed to raise their capital and operating expenses from capital markets. On the other hand, partially commercialised SOEs are expected to at least cover their operating costs (Nellis and Kikeri 1989; Nellis and Shirley 1991).

The operations of some SOEs might require a high level of capital investment, in which case the government has to intervene. In some cases, commercialisation could involve the change of the relationship between the management of the SOE and the government through performance or management contracts.

Performance contracts are used to define new relationships between the management of SOEs and the government with a view to making the achievement of desired results possible. On the other hand, under management contracts, management of the SOE is taken up by a private enterprise in exchange for a fee payable by the government (Shirley 1983, 1989; Nellis and Kikeri 1989).

Unlike privatisation, commercialisation does not involve any alteration in state ownership and control; ownership is still vested in the state. Some state-owned enterprises (SOEs), which are referred to as 'strategic' such as water and electricity, have been retained by governments in Africa, and not divested to private ownership. These enterprises have been subjected to commercialisation, the essence of which is to expose the enterprises to market forces so as to make them operate as profit-making commercial ventures.

Some of the measures of commercialisation include: price liberalisation, whereby price controls are lifted and price increases or tariffs of good and services provided by the SOEs are permitted; the removal of barriers to the entry of private firms so that the latter can compete with the SOEs; wide discretion given to managers of SOEs to determine tariffs, hire and fire employees and make investment decisions; and the introduction of performance contracts and performance evaluation systems (Tangri 1999; Cowan 1990; Ramanadham 1989).

Reasons for Privatisation or Commercialisation

The growing appeal of privatisation and commercialisation stems from an ideology of neoclassical economics, which desires less government intervention in the economy, and believes in the superior economic performance of the private sector. According to this theory, a free-market economy, without state intervention, will lead to economic prosperity that will 'trickle down' to the poorest members of society. Therefore, government interference in the economy is considered unnecessary and harmful, because it acts as a brake on economic progress.

Privatisation and commercialisation were developed within this framework of neoclassical economic theory that advocates liberalisation of the economy and circumspection of the role of the state in the economy (Ramanadham 1989; Butler 1985; Cowan 1990; Nellis and Kikeri 1989; Bienen and Waterbury 1989). The history of the economic policies determining privatisation and commercialisation can be traced back over the past three decades. During this period nations in various parts of the world have sporadically implemented privatisation and commercialisation as instruments of development strategy. For instance, in 1966, after the overthrow of the Nkrumah government, the National Liberation Council government, under the influence of the World Bank policy, privatised a number of state enterprises (Ayee 1990; Tangri 1991; Gyimah-Boadi 1991; Adda 1989; Ayee 1994).

However, the introduction of privatisation and commercialisation on a massive scale is of comparatively recent origin, being first introduced in Britain under Margaret Thatcher in the early 1980s; and from there proliferating into developing countries, including Africa.

However, although privatisation and commercialisation in Africa are influenced by neoclassical ideology, the decision to embark upon the two programmes is due to some external and internal factors. For example, some African countries view privatisation and commercialisation as means of raising government revenue. Countries, which have acute financial problems, are quick to resort to privatisation and commercialisation to reduce their fiscal and credit pressures. Mainly for this reason, Guinea, for instance, raised US$770,000 from the sale of fourteen public enterprises (Young 1991).

Pressure on Africa countries to privatise and commercialise state enterprises also comes from external sources: African countries must privatise and commercialise their state enterprises in order to qualify for the stabilisation and structural adjustment loans provided by the World Bank and IMF. Whenever countries refuse to accept this prescription, the Bretton Woods institutions deny them financial assistance. The structural adjustment programme, the buzzword of the 1980s and 1990s, requires the reduction of government deficit through austerity measures including the reduction of government expenditure. For example, the privatisation programmes undertaken in Ghana, Togo, Guinea, Uganda and other African countries have been at least in part due to pressure from the Bretton Woods institutions.

Three main arguments have been advanced for privatisation and commercialisation. First, it is argued that it is an over-extended state structure that distorts development; and therefore that the role of the state in the economy of African countries should be limited, and its activities rolled back.

However, this argument ignores the reasons for the growth of the role of the public sector in the economy of African countries in the first place. The active role of the state was necessary to redirect internal economic activity, to protect indigenous enterprises against multinational monopolies, and to redefine the position of the African countries economy within the global economy. Specific social and economic problems required state intervention in general, and the formation of public enterprises in particular (Ghai 1991; Ramanadham 1995).

Secondly, the justification for privatisation and commercialisation policies is that state enterprises have failed to generate an investable surplus, having instead created a budgetary burden for the public sector. Therefore, it is argued that privatising and commercialisation these enterprises and exposing them to the discipline of the market would make them efficient and profitable (Ramanadham 1989; Shirley 1989; Cowan 1990).

Third, the argument for privatisation and commercialisation is related to the issue of democracy. In view of the authoritarian nature of most African states and their weak economic performance, some observers believe that privatisation and commercialisation could enhance the democratisation process, and promote sustainable development on the African continent (Dorraj 1994). However, the question, that should be asked, is: what kind of democracy?

Democracy is a universal concept with a value judgement attached to it. If democracy is understood to imply social equality, the fair distribution of income and empowering the poor, then privatisation and commercialisation are certainly not the answer. In the African context, democracy cannot be understood in terms of liberal or authoritarian democracy, but rather in terms of popular democracy (Shivji 1991; Kumssa 1996).

Privatisation and Commercialisation: A Performance Appraisal

Shirley and Nellis (1991) have cautioned that the performance of privatisation should not be measured by the number of transactions, the price paid, or whether or not an enterprise survives. Rather, the test of privatisation is whether the transaction yields a net benefit to the economy as a whole. Since privatisation is a relatively new strategy, African countries may not have all the necessary conditions for its success. Nevertheless, it is possible to evaluate the performance of privatisation and commercialisation based on the record in African countries since the mid-1980s, especially in Ghana, which is reputed to have implemented far-reaching privatisation programmes.

The record of privatisation and commercialisation in Africa has been patchy, slow, modest, and therefore unimpressive. Admittedly, a few countries such as Ghana, Zambia and Uganda have vigorously pursued privatisation, while a majority of the countries including Senegal, Tunisia, Benin, Côte d'Ivoire, Togo, Cameroon, Kenya, Guinea and Nigeria have either made modest or limited progress, or reversed privatisation policies at periodic intervals (Lalaye 1999). Other countries such as South Africa, Zimbabwe and Tanzania have remained strongly tied to public ownership. They have therefore taken limited steps towards privatisation and commercialisation because of their leaders' strong attachment to state capitalism.

At first glance, privatisation efforts appear to have been moderately successful. Almost all countries have managed to halt the increase in SOEs. Several have reduced their number. Throughout Africa, reform has led to the privatisation of mostly small and medium-sized, but also a few large SOEs.

Among the adjusting countries, governments have divested themselves of over 700 firms — less than a quarter of the total number of SOEs — either by their holdings or by liquidating non-viable SOEs. There has been a slightly greater number of privatisations than liquidations. Progress has been uneven (see Table 6). Six countries — Ghana, Guinea, Nigeria, Benin, Mozambique, Benin and Senegal — account for two-thirds of the divestitures. Only a handful of countries have divested more than 40 per cent of their enterprises. And half the countries have been extremely slow to privatise any enterprises. In Kenya, for example, there have been almost no sales in ten years. A few countries have even expanded their SOEs. In Burundi, the SOE sector grew during the adjustment period, with five firms divested, but twelve new ones created. In Côte d'Ivoire, the number of SOEs rose from 113 in 1922 to 140 in 1990, despite the privatisation of some thirty SOEs in the mid-1980s (World Bank 1995a).

More importantly, the number of divestitures overstates the extent of privatisation. Large SOEs with the bulk of public assets — airlines, railroads, mining and utilities — have generally not been privatised, even though this has changed. Ghana, for instance, privatised its gold and diamond mines, a brewery and several medium-sized manufacturing units. Nigeria sold several hotels and a gasoline distribution company to private investors. In most countries, including most of those where the government sold many firms, the focus on small and medium-sized SOEs means that the size of the SOE sector overall has hardly changed. The four SOEs sold in Côte d'Ivoire in 1991 accounted for a mere 0.1 per cent of the government's holdings. Possible exceptions are Benin, Guinea and Nigeria, where reportedly some 5 to 15 per cent of government shareholdings have been privatised (World Bank 1995a).

Further complicating the picture are problems with the data (Berg 1993). Sometimes SOEs are reported as sold, when they are merely up for sale. Sometimes sales are recorded, when the privatisation agency and a buyer reach a preliminary agreement; even though the deal later falls apart. For instance, of the twenty-one SOEs listed as privatised in the 1991 report of Ghana's Divestiture Implementation Committee, eleven were returned to the state's portfolio in 1992. Furthermore, government data do not distinguish between the various types of transactions. The sale of a 3 per cent government holding in a company largely under private ownership is treated in the same way as the full privatisation of a company that was completely government-owned.

Moreover, a sale might turn out to involve the transfer of assets from one SOE to another. Such transactions include Mali's sale of a publicly owned vegetable oil mill to another SOE; and Ghana's purported privatisation of the Achimota Brewery Limited, when in fact 45 per cent of the equity was transferred from the government to publicly owned banks and insurance companies. Such liquidations are mere fictions, in that the firms had long since ceased to operate (World Bank 1995a, 1995b, 2002).

Political and Administrative Factors

A combination of political and economic factors has been identified as contributing to the slow progress of privatisation in Africa.

Cook and Minogue (1990) have postulated that non-economic, political and administrative factors affect the content and implementation of privatisation and commercialisation programmes. The point has been reinforced by the World Bank (1995a:1) that 'privatisation is always political'; and that successful privatisation and commercialisation must be politically desirable to leaders and constituencies; politically feasible for leaders to implement; and politically credible to investors and to other affected constituencies (World Bank 1995b).

It is therefore, not surprising that privatisation and commercialisation programmes in Africa have been politically controversial. Because of the highly political and sensitive nature of such programmes, African governments have generally been cautious in implementing them. Tangri (1999) has shown that in the 1990s, when Ghana had over 200 SOEs, the Rawlings government was prepared to privatise only twenty SOEs annually. Similarly, in Kenya, where there were 300 SOEs, Daniel Arap Moi's Kenya African National Union (KANU) government divested only ten SOEs per year.

Table 6: Privatisation of SOEs in Africa 1986–2002

% of SOEs divested	No. of enterprises before divestiture			
	0–50	51–100	101–200	More than 200
0–10	The Gambia Mauritania Rwanda Sierra Leone Zimbabwe	Burkina Faso Congo Braz. Uganda Zambia	Cameroon Côte d'Ivoire Malawi	Kenya Tanzania
11–25	Chad	Burundi CAR	Madagascar	Ghana Mozambique
26–40	Niger		Guinea Nigeria	
41–60	Guinea-Bissau	Benin Mali Senegal Togo		

Sources: World Bank 1995a, 1995b, 2002; Adamolekun 1999.

Another political and administrative factor is labour union pressure against privatisation, because of the massive retrenchment exercise that normally accompanies it. This was the case in Nigeria, Ghana, Senegal and Kenya. For instance, Senegal's privatisation, which started in 1987, faced institutional and political obstacles: 'trade union activism and public opinion have been influential in the postponement of privatization policies. Fear of employee redundancies, price hikes and suspicion as the promised benefits have created an air of hostility which has, in some cases, led to riots' (Caulfield 2006: 19).

Another factor is bureaucratic resistance from the managers of SOEs, who feel that they would lose their positions and perquisites they enjoy. Privatisation poses a threat to an important source of patronage for politicians. This diminution in patronage must been seen vis-à-vis the implementation of structural adjustment programmes, which were aimed at eliminating opportunities for patronage in political and economic arenas. Consequently, politicians were naturally unwilling to embark on massive privatisation of SOEs, which would reduce their source of political patronage.

Ideologically, privatisation has been popular with leaders who have inclined towards socialism, such as Robert Mugabe of Zimbabwe and Ali Hassan Mwinyi of Tanzania, who felt that state capitalism offered the best guarantee for building a fairer, more humane and egalitarian society.

81

Privatisation has often aroused vocal nationalist sentiments, because foreign private companies, promoted by privatisation, are seen as antithetical to national interests. Such sentiments have been aroused in Zimbabwe and Zambia, and most particularly in Kenya, where Asian, and even local Kikuyu, businessmen were viewed as the prime beneficiaries of privatisation. In the case of Senegal, 'the control and operation of such enterprises is often politically charged...privatization does not remove the political nature of these activities, and may do little do ease the involvement of politicians in key sectoral decisions' (Bayliss 2003: 508). In the case of Guinea, a breakdown of contract arrangements with a private provider, allegedly due to excessive pricing, led to a threatened re-nationalisation (Bayliss 2003).

Finally, there has not been much popular backing for privatisation because of the perception that it neither improves income distribution, nor creates new jobs (Tangri 1999; World Bank 1995a, 1995b; Turner and Hulme 1997).

Economic Factors

Economic factors posing an obstacle to the realisation of the objectives of privatisation and commercialisation include the lack of public resources to pay the outstanding liabilities of the divested SOEs, including the payment of high severance packages for retrenched employees; and determining the valuation of the public assets for sale. A classic example is the privatisation of Zambia's two biggest copper mines in 1998, which ran into serious difficulties because the offer from the group of mining consortia was felt to be below the expectations of the government.

Given the limited development of an indigenous private sector, it is difficult to find buyers with the requisite capital to acquire the big SOEs. The unwillingness of prospective buyers to invest in most SOEs is because of their poor financial and material conditions, their physical location, and buyers' preference for readily available profitable forms of investment. It is difficult to assess early on in advance the profitability of privatised SOEs in a largely competitive and turbulent business environment (Suleiman and Waterbury 1990; Tangri 1999; World Bank 1995a, 1995b).

In short, limited privatisation has had little impact on efficiency and economic growth. In some cases, a government has continued to hold a major share — and to intervene — in a partly privatised firm. In other cases, severance benefits to dismissed employees were so large that governments had to siphon public resources away from productive use. Many privatisations did not lead to greater efficiency, because the new owners received favours — tax benefits, duty-free imports, tariff protection, priority access to credit and other scarce inputs — that reduced social benefits. Where governments allowed buyers to defer payments, speculative buyers, who were unqualified to run the SOEs, sometimes bought them, hoping to resell for a quick profit. Pressure on governments to sell may also have led to ill-considered transactions. And cronyism and corruption have undercut privatisation benefits. Transactions in Ghana, Guinea and Nigeria, for example, have been criticised for their lack of transparency (Berg 1993; World Bank 2002).

Positive Cases of Privatisation

In spite of the poor record of privatisation in most African states, there are some positive cases. In Uganda, for instance, privatisation allowed Shell International to diversify product lines, and upgrade and rehabilitate facilities. Specifically, it enabled Shell to concentrate on core activities, and to contract out the non-core activities. Actual investment far exceeded the requirement under the privatisation deal to invest US$10,000,000 over three years. In just two years US$13,000,000 was invested in new and rehabilitated filling stations. Similarly, in Kenya, privatisation led to improvement in the financial performance of the Housing Finance Company, privatised in 1992. Its profits increased by more than 100 per cent between 1992 and 1993. Addition to these two successful cases, management changes and new investments associated with privatisation led to improvements in the performance of Lever International, when it acquired a majority stake in Unilever Ghana Ltd. Its shareholding increased from 45 to 70 per cent, and gave Lever International the necessary flexibility on matters relating to strategic direction, capital investment, mergers and acquisitions. The investment reduced unit costs and increased production by 50 per cent without increasing energy consumption (African Development Bank 2005).

The Ghanaian Experience of Privatisation

The record of privatisation and commercialisation in Africa can be demonstrated with evidence from the Ghanaian experience, which has arguably undertaken a far-reaching privatisation programme. Initial progress in implementing divestiture was slow. The first sale was concluded in 1990. This could be attributed to the weight of technical, informational and organisational difficulties. Divestment is technically one of the most difficult of all structural adjustment measures. Diverse skills are needed, and Ghana found it difficult to attract the requi-

83

site high-level technical personnel. A paucity of data available on the SOEs, as well as on problems of identifying and valuing assets and liabilities, militated against the speedy implementation of the divestiture programme. The legal procedures to liquidate SOEs proved unduly lengthy. And the use of a foreign consultancy firm proved unsatisfactory; the contract with Price Waterhouse was cancelled (Ayee 1990; Ayee 1994b; Tangri 1991; Gyimah-Boadi 1991).

These difficulties notwithstanding, the prime obstacle to slow implementation of divestiture has been identified as political: 'Politics has influenced what state enterprises are to be divested, and to whom, as well as on what terms. And the politics itself has been influenced by previous attempts at divestiture' (Tangri 1991:528).

However, since 1992 the pace of divestiture has increased, because most of the technical, informational and organisational – and even the political – difficulties had been overcome. As of December 1998, a total of 212 SOEs were divested through various means, principally the sale of assets and shares, joint ventures, liquidations and leasing (Table 7).

Table 7: Divestiture of State-owned Enterprises, 1991–1998

Mode	1988–1991	1992	1993	1994	1995	1996	1997	1998	Total
Sale of assets	16	4	3	30	19	18	15	7	112
Sale of shares	11	5	2	2	6	1	2	2	31
Joint venture	6	3	1	4	0	4	1	2	21
Lease	3	1	0	1	0	0	1	0	6
Liquidation	24	2	5	5	6	0	0	0	42
Total	60	15	11	42	31	23	19	11	212

Source: Divestiture Implementation Committee, Accra, 2000.

In 1994, the Ghanaian government decided to accelerate the divestiture programme. In April 1994, it raised around US$350,000,000 from the divestment of 25 per cent of its shares in Ashanti Goldfields Corporation, the country's most profitable mining company; and a further US$23,000,000 from the sale of its stake in seven manufacturing companies – Lever Brothers, Enterprise Insurance Company, Pioneer Tobacco Company, Guinness, Ghana Ltd, and Nestle, Ghana Ltd – listed on the Ghana Stock Exchange (Dordunoo 1997; World Bank 1996).

In January 1995, the government announced that it would sell a further 114 enterprises. In late 1995 and 1996, the government successfully floated two state-owned banks, Ghana Commercial Bank (GCB) and the Agricultural Development Bank (ADB), on the stock exchange, and advertised the sale of a strategic stake in Ghana Telecom (Ayee 1998).

Proceeds from the divestiture transactions amounted to US$ 909.617 billion, equivalent to about 13.98 per cent of the mean GDP 1988–1998. A considerable share of about US$454,000,000, representing about 47.75 per cent of the total divestiture proceeds, was derived from the sale of the Ashanti Goldfield Company alone. According to Appiah-Kubi (2001), total gross sales proceeds, as reflected in the total purchase of state-owned enterprises divested by the Divestiture Implementation Committee (DIC), was about US$268.9 billion, as against total receipts to date of about US$193.9 billion. This leaves about US$84.9 billion claims on divested enterprises yet to be settled by purchasers. Part of the receipts from divestiture transactions were used to settle employee entitlements, consisting of accumulated salary arrears, severance payments and other liabilities, including debts owed to the creditors of divested enterprises.

According to Appiah-Kubi (2001), Ghana's privatisation programme compares in magnitude and impact with the much-discussed privatisation programmes of Latin America. Despite having started very late, Ghana's privatisation programme shows an impressive record, both in the volume and value of divestitures, as compared with sub-Saharan Africa as a whole. Between 1989 and 1999, over 70 per cent, about 212, of Ghana's state-owned enterprises from all sectors, including some very large enterprises, were sold, liquidated or otherwise disposed off. This resulted in partial or complete withdrawal of the government from a range of sectors, leading to a significant reduction in the government's direct engagement in the economy. Gross proceeds from privatisation transactions were equivalent to about 13.94 per cent of mean GDP in 1989–1999. This magnitude alone is sufficient to account for the relative success of the programme. To Appiah-Kubi:

> Contributing to this relative success is also the inter-linkage of the divestiture programme with other economic reforms: macroeconomic stabilization, trade liberalization, deregulation, and domestic and foreign investment drive (Appiah-Kubi 2001: 211).

However, the fact still remains that not all SOEs slated for divestiture have been sold, even though it may be conceded that privatisation is a long and continuous process that depends on the identification of the right buyer (Dordunoo 1997). A classic example of an SOE that has not been sold is the State Fishing Corporation, which was among the first list of 30 SOEs slated for divestiture in 1988.

To make the divestiture process more effective and to make information more readily available to interested parties, the government approved and published new divestiture procedures in 1995. On its part, the DIC prepared a comprehensive manual, setting out in detail how the new procedures would be operationalised. The manual deals with the preparation of documentation, advertising, bidding procedures, evaluation criteria and procedures, negotiation and approvals, sale and purchase documentation, and completion and post-completion matters.

One important mechanism that appears to have accelerated the pace of the divestiture programme is outsourcing the sale of SOEs to private firms. This began in 1996. The procedures manual specifies arrangements for outsourcing. A register of firms was prepared by the DIC, following public advertisement internationally and locally. With outsourcing, it is envisaged that the rate of divestiture will rise to an expected annual rate of twenty-five to thirty-five medium and large enterprises. Not less than 50 per cent of the firms' remuneration will be represented by success fees to be paid from the proceeds of sale. Proposed credit would finance retainer fees and firms' reimbursable expenses (World Bank 1996).

The benefits of outsourcing are enormous. First, they allow the DIC to accelerate the pace of divestiture by utilising private sector resources and expertise. Second, with the appropriate financial and success fee incentives in place, private sector privatisation specialists, with hands-on experience in negotiating sale transactions, are more likely to secure quality investors, and increased sales proceeds in a timely manner. Thirdly, openness and access to information concerning the divestiture process is enhanced. Fourthly, outsourcing fosters development of private services sector in Ghana through the direct use of local consultants, lawyers and financial advisory firms to undertake divestitures, and through the skills transfer arising from associations between local and international firms.

However, the supposed benefits of outsourcing have not been realised in the Ghanaian experience. This is because the costs of the divestiture process have also increased as a result of the outsourcing programme. According to the DIC, the outsourcing programme has been a complete failure. After signing around 21 outsourcing contracts and spending US$1,800,000 in fixed consultant fees, the programme has been able to produce only two completed divestitures in three years (Appiah-Kubi 2001).

Moreover, although Ghana's privatisation programme has achieved some success, it may be described as a failure if measured against indices of performance such as: the numbers of enterprises divested (analysed in categories of small, medium and large); by the mode of divestiture; the number of divestitures out-sourced; the net proceeds on divestiture; the level of deferred payments and arrears arising under deferred payments (individual and aggregate); and the average time taken to divest enterprises.

Major Obstacles to Accelerated Privatisation

A number of major obstacles to privatisation have been encountered. First, participation by Ghanaian businessmen, managers, employees, institutional and individual investors and the public at large in the divestiture programme has been limited. This is partially due to the absence of a fully functioning capital market in the country. The government has sought to facilitate local ownership through a system of deferred payments for share of asset sales. However, the system has been implemented on an ad hoc basis. Problems have arisen with its administration, in particular, in relation to the collection of deferred balances.

Second, labour issues have been handled on an ad hoc basis. The entitlements of junior employees are normally recorded in collective bargaining agreements (CBAs). Senior employees and management have negotiated similar or more generous agreements. But their standing appears less certain, as these agreements are not recognised as CBAs, having been effectively negotiated by senior employees themselves. While there is no explicit policy, and some inconsistency in application from enterprise to enterprise, a general pattern has emerged showing that rates of payments for junior staff have been in the range of six to fifteen months, mostly within the range of eight to ten months, of salary, irrespective of the length of service (World Bank 1996). Similar payments have been made in respect of senior staff, although more generous provisions had sometimes been negotiated. Profitable enterprises pay somewhat higher severance packages that weaker ones, although ability to pay is generally not a factor in negotiating CBAs.

Thirdly, there is no reliable estimate of the potential liability severance and termination payments arising from the divestiture programme. Rough estimates are that up to 40,000 employees may be affected, at a cost of around US$40,000,000. This compares with over 60,000 redundancies from the civil service reform programme, and around 100,000 in the Cocoa Marketing Board in the late 1980s and early 1990s. The divestiture programme has therefore made the government captive to massive liabilities, as a result of the payment of terminal benefits, which, given the weak financial position of some SOEs — for some, liabilities exceed the value of their assets — they are unable to meet.

Fourthly, there is evidence that the behaviour of both management and workers changes, once the intention to privatise an enterprise is announced. There is therefore need to take immediate action, even before the sale process commences, in such areas as: forbidding the renegotiation of existing CBAs without the government's approval; instituting a complete freeze on recruitment; ensuring that all social security payments are up to date; identifying the potential level of redundancies; and preparing the labour input for the divestiture strategy (Ayee 1998).

Other obstacles to privatisation in Ghana have included: SOEs with excess assets and onerous liabilities; inadequate management in the SOEs to be divested; lack of management competence of local entrepreneurs buying the SOEs; excessive levels of employees; valuation and selling price; absence of information about the SOEs; legal constraints, especially where the laws are made from a foreign context; use of other divestiture implementation agencies other than the DIC, especially in the divestiture of eight companies on the Ghana Stock Exchange and of the financial institutions by Financial Sector Adjustment Programme (FINSAP) Secretariat; a lack of transparency; problems of deferred payments, systems and procedures, especially in the absence of computerised database; and a resistance to divestiture by the Trades Union Congress, as a result of the massive lay off of workers envisaged under divestiture (Agbodo 1994; Dordunoo 1997).

Lessons of Privatisation in Ghana for the African Continent

There is no doubt that Ghana's privatisation programme has achieved limited success. It has placed too much emphasis on public finance rationalisation and faith in the market system. Socio-political and regulatory issues have been neglected. The privatisation programme has led to job losses, while ownership of assets has shifted in the favour of foreigners. It has not created an environment inducive to indigenous private investment, because little attention was given to the regulation of the commercial activities of privatised businesses. Even though the programme is judged to have achieved its fiscal adjustment goal, it has not been able to achieve the many objectives for which it was implemented.

Notwithstanding these criticisms, Appiah-Kubi has high a regard for the achievement of Ghana's privatisation programme. In his view:

> ...as the total benefits of a privatization programme are not judged only on its short term effects, the Ghanaian privatization programme should not be seen as a flop. At least it has contributed towards stabilizing the macro-economy, and helped bring about a change in the economic structure of Ghana, which until recently was characterized by financially distressed state-owned enterprises, plagued in many cases by excessive

political interference, poor management and high degree of protection as against the private sector Appiah-Kubi (2001: 225).

Other experiences and lessons from the Ghanaian implementation of privatisation are summarised below.

The privatisation programme, designed to achieve budgetary benefits, has the potential of becoming a substantial fiscal burden because of the huge capital outlay involved in the payment of severance or terminal benefits. Unless the government considers the trade-offs between objectives before taking action, it can make costly errors.

Many sales programmes have focused on the short-run revenue effects, but long-run net fiscal benefits are by no means assured; if say, the sales price of a profitable firm plus the present value of future tax revenues are less than the present value of the net future income stream under state ownership, the sale worsens the government's financial position.

Even while it eliminates a fiscal drain on the government, the sale or lease of an unprofitable firm can leave the economy worse off if extensive concessions have to be extended to the buyer. For example, short-run revenue gains may be maximised by selling monopolies, but the failure to exploit opportunities for competition – such as trade reform, breaking up monopolies, and ending special privileges – can impose considerable long-run costs on the economy; not only must downstream firms and final consumers pay higher prices if a monopoly is kept in place, but the absence of competitive pressure allows new technologies and markets to be neglected. These circumstances suggest that the selection of a particular method of privatisation – liquidation, contracting for activities previously handled within government, leases and management contracts, sales through private placement, competitive bidding, and share issues – should be conditioned on the government's objectives, the condition of the SOEs, and the circumstances of the country (Vuylsteke 1988; Nellis and Shirley 1991).

The success of privatisation is dependent on the size, experience, economic health, and viability of the private sector. In countries where the private sector is very small and corrupt, there is little chance of success. The UN commission's report on Africa, for example, concludes that privatisation in Africa is impossible

...because the private sector is simply not capable of taking over the functions now performed by SOEs. Moreover, the policy reforms leading to market-controlled prices demanded by structural adjustment lending and privatization will result in increased poverty at the lower end of the social scale, while serving to enrich the new entrepreneurs that are a result of them (Cowan 1990:10).

Proponents of privatisation argue that high taxation of profitable private enterprises will help the government to expand its services to the poorest sectors of the population and prevent profound social inequality.

An important challenge for all governments pursuing privatisation is to develop and manage effectively the processes and procedures for transferring SOEs to private ownership and for eliciting the participation of the private sector in providing public services and infrastructure. Experience suggests that government actions needed to expand private sector participation include: enacting adequate legal reforms to allow the private sector to operate efficiently and effectively; developing procedures that are clear and transparent to potential investments and other private sector participants; removing unnecessary restrictions and regulations on private enterprises that limit their ability to compete in the market; and allowing for liquidation or bankruptcy of SOEs that cannot be commercialised or privatised. It may also be necessary to expand opportunities for private enterprises to develop management capabilities, create incentives and assurances to protect current state employees, and reform and restructure SOEs that cannot be sold immediately (Rondinelli and Iacono 1996).

The ultimate success of privatisation is dependent upon cooperation of the public and private sectors, a well-conceived economic policy, and adept political leadership, which would provide incentive, direction and guidance. In other words, successful privatisation requires the commitment of both political and business leaders to encourage the expansion of the private sector as an instrument of economic and social development.

Although privatisation is an essential instrument for transforming government-controlled economies into market-oriented systems, and for making established market economies more efficient, it is neither a panacea for all government's ills, nor sufficient to ensure economic progress. Privatisation is most effective as part of a broader programme of economic policy reforms and institutional development. The advantages of privatisation can be maximised when government assumes a competitive environment, has adequate procedures for promoting cost reduction and service quality, strongly supports small- and medium-scale enterprise development and SOE restructuring, and performs an effective regulatory role to minimise corruption and inequity.

Privatisation should be viewed, not as an end in itself, but as part of a broader programme of reforms designed to promote a better allocation of resources, encourage competition, foster a supportive environment for entrepreneurial development, and develop the capital market. Divestitures that follow, or parallel macroeconomic and institutional reforms, have shown very much better outcomes than operations undertaken in isolation from such reforms. Although this view may seem obvious, the pace of privatisation has not always been well orchestrated with the removal of distortions and the development of a supportive institutional, managerial and financial environment.

Privatisation requires special administrators. Managing a privatisation programme is a complex matter; and government officials seldom have the requisite skills. Moreover, the government may be in a weak bargaining position: it may be publicly committed to privatisation, but burdened by unattractive enterprises, and short on the information and experience required to make good deals. A common outcome in such circumstances is that assets are undervalued and offered with unduly favourable financing. To overcome these weaknesses, some sort of central administrative unit must oversee the privatisation process and keep decision-makers informed (Nellis and Shirley 1991). In a nutshell, privatisation should not be regarded as simply a

> [t]echnical matter of introducing private sector medicine to the ailing public sector patient. The interplay of political forces must be taken into account in designing and implementing public sector reforms. Care must be taken to attempt what is feasible and not simply shoot for impossible goals. Strategies must incorporate consideration of the attitudes and actions of interested parties. What is technically possible is not necessarily what is politically feasible (Turner and Hulme 1997:198).

Corporate Plans, Performance Contracts and Non-privatised SOEs

Four actions are needed to enable the government to reform its relationships with SOEs, which have not been privatised: the setting of clear and attainable objectives compatible with the commercial operation of the SOE; giving management greater autonomy over the operation of the SOE and selection of managers capable of operating independently; establishing clear rules, procedures, and limits for government involvement in decision-making; holding managers accountable by negotiating targets, monitoring and evaluating results, and rewarding managers and staff on the basis of performance (Nellis and Shirley 1992; Nellis 1989). Two partly complementary means of addressing these action areas are corporate plans, sometimes called strategic plans, and performance contracts.

Corporate Plans

Most African countries have asked their SOEs, which have not been privatised, to develop internally formulated corporate plans. Corporate plans have been regarded as not only an 'instrument for promoting the effectiveness and efficiency of SOEs and upgrading their performance levels...but also the most pragmatic way of establishing a bridge between the government and the SOE' (Fernandes 1986).

A corporate plan involves six main elements: defining the mission of the SOE; designing long-term strategies; developing functional plans; dealing with interlinkages; defining SOE-state relationships; and articulating the performance evaluation criteria (Fernandes 1986; Nellis 1989; Nellis and Shirley 1991).

Ideally, a corporate plan analyses the business environment of the SOE, assesses how it is likely to change, and enunciates goals and strategies for the future. It includes targets, benchmarks for monitoring achievement, and an investment programme. Although the plan may be a means of negotiating objectives with government, its primary purpose is to enunciate management's vision of the future course of the SOE. Thus, the plan becomes part of the culture of the SOE and is reflected in its annual budgets and investment projects (Ayee 1994c).

In the public sector in Africa, corporate planning by SOEs has often proved fruitless, as it requires management with independence, continuity and commitment. Managers of SOEs face a number of disincentives and obstacles to adapting to medium-term changes in their environment through corporate plans or through other means because

...the market [of SOEs] is protected and their prices controlled, subsidies or loans are readily available to pay for past mistakes, and the penalty for failure is remote; frequent rotation of managers, directors, and supervisors reduces the commitment to long-term needs; and the government's social welfare aims may take precedence over the long-term health of the enterprises. These obstacles have led many observers to recommend that the state particularly avoid, or divest ownership in, 'entrepreneurial' industries in which dynamic adaptation to changing consumer tastes is paramount, such as electronics (Nellis and Shirley 1991:28).

Performance Contracts

Performance contracts, also called contract plans, have an advantage over corporate plans in both the dialogue they generate between the SOE and the government, and in the two-way nature of the obligations they create. Under performance contracts, governments pledge to meet their financial and other obligations to the SOE, and to renounce ad hoc interference. In exchange, the SOE accepts negotiated performance targets. These have become mechanisms or devices aimed not only at improving the effectiveness and efficiency of SOEs but also as a means of 'bridging the autonomy-accountability conundrum between the government and public enterprises' (Islam 1993:139). Spelling out the rights and duties of the SOEs and the government, they were devised to attack vague objectives, insufficient autonomy and weak incentives. Senegal was the first sub-Saharan African country to implement performance contracts in the early 1980s. By 2000, over thirty countries had either signed or were drafting over 120 contracts, absorbing millions of dollars worth of technical assistance from donors (World Bank 2002).

Although contracts can be useful in identifying problems facing an SOE, they generally have not been effective in improving the performance of key SOEs. For instance, in the case of Senegal, performance contracts did not work as intended, in part, because the government not only 'did not provide promised resources, but it also failed consistently to pay its bills, even when the funds were earmarked in the budgets of various agencies for this purpose' (Islam 1993:1131-2). Other problems with the contract plan were weak review agencies, inefficient budgeting systems, lack of reliable data, economic malaise and poverty (Nellis 1989; Caulfield 2006).

A few countries report, however, some success. In Mauritania and The Gambia, the governments agreed to make appropriate budget allocations for water and electricity, helping to ailing utilities back on to their feet. In Cameroon, where the government signed contracts with major utilities, neither the government nor the utilities have lived up to their obligations and the contracts have had little in impact. In Ghana, only four of the eleven firms with performance contracts reached the negotiated targets, because of the lack of financial discipline and performance accountability (Ayee 1994c).

In pursuance of the aim of the reform programmes to improve performance management in the civil service in Africa, performance agreements have also been introduced as a means of assessing and measuring the performance of senior civil servants. The objective of the performance agreements is to ensure that senior officials are 'output oriented', and that they can be held accountable by the government for the delivery of specific outputs. In Ghana, agreements were first introduced for chief directors in January 1997; and then subsequently formally launched at a ceremony presided over by the country's vice president in June 1997. Following an evaluation in early 1998, the scheme was extended in

1999 to cover over 250 other senior officials: directors, heads of departments, and coordinating directors of the metropolitan, municipal and district assemblies (Dodoo 1998).

According to Nellis and Shirley (1991), making a performance contract work may require conditions that seldom exist. First, the contract system should be a part, rather than the foundation, of any reform effort. Before any contracts are negotiated, the government and the SOE should agree on general principles of operation. The SOE should develop a vision of its future and a corporate strategy that fits the government's macroeconomic strategy. When introduced, the process should be recognised as experimental.

Second, at the outset, governments should choose an SOE that is not operating in a competitive environment, and that is not in a desperate financial condition. SOEs operating in a competitive market without a heavy social service burden usually do not need contracts. They should be privatised, or, if that is not acceptable, regulated by the market with minimal government supervision of investments and debt. And although governments typically wish to apply contracts to their poorest performers, the French experience, confirmed in Africa, is that the weaker the SOE, the harder the negotiation of a contract will be.

Third, the contract's stipulation of payments from the government to the SOEs is often unrealistic, given the financial constraints on governments. Often, governments do not bargain in good faith. A government's subsequent failure to honour its financial obligations calls the entire contract into question. The lack of realism and faith is hard to overcome, but contracts, as is the case of some in Senegal, may try to do so by identifying the services that will be suspended in the case of non-payment.

The negotiation of the contract should be part of the government's budget process. When it is not, the contract is in jeopardy of being disregarded in budget decisions. Negotiating outside of the budget process places a heavy burden on management. To ensure that the agreements reached in the contract are honoured elsewhere in government, other decision makers, especially the minister of finance, must be party to the negotiations, or be otherwise bound by the contract.

Contracts, especially initial ones, should be limited in scope and provisional. In Africa, where the financial and economic situation is far weaker and more uncertain than in France, contracts have of necessity remained more detailed and complex. Both parties must be committed. Some recapitalisation is usually part of a restructuring programme. And there must be enforceable targets, incentives for success, and censure or financial punishments for failure. Lacking these essentials, governments and SOEs have often disregarded carefully negotiated provisions, and have failed to make necessary management changes in the enterprises, and to deliver promised financial resources. Similarly, SOEs have avoided difficult financial and personnel restructuring measures. So the considerable time, effort and resources spent developing performance contracts have achieved relatively little. Perhaps most disturbingly, attention may have to be diverted from more fundamental reforms such as divestiture (Ayee 1994c).

Public-Private Partnerships

Public-private partnerships (PPPs)[1] are the most recent privatisation reform initiatives to have emerged in Africa. Even though state and non-state actors in Africa have worked together for centuries to solve societal problems, partnerships between the two sectors have become a much more powerful tool in the twenty-first century, because of the redefinition of the role of the state. The economic crises of the late 1970s and 1980s, and the lessons of international experience from the success of market-friendly economies, have combined to force a redefinition of the role of the state:

> The boundaries between the state and the market have been redrawn, with important activities that used to be an integral part of state activity now in the hands of non-state actors, for and not-for-profit alike. At the same time the state sector is transforming itself continuously by rearranging the assignment of responsibilities, most notably through the decentralization of functions to local and regional governments and subcontracting specific functions to non-state actors (Fiszbein 2000: 163)

A public-private partnership is defined as a broad range of arrangements that involve a combination of state and non-state actors in the fulfilment of traditional state functions such as health, water, education, sanitation and citizen security, as a result of the redefinition of the role of the state (Batley 1996; Fiszbein and Lowden 1999). The common denominator of a partnership is the 'pooling of resources (financial, human, technical and intangibles such as information and political support) from public and private sources to achieve a commonly agreed social goal' (Fiszbein 2000: 164).

Advocates of public-private partnerships suggest an impressive list of possible benefits and advantages. They are said to promote: improved responsiveness to public need and greater performance orientation; expansion in the quantity and quality of public goods and services that can be produced beyond the level possible under pure private or public arrangements; and the strengthening of partners in a number of ways, so as to make them more effective in their own endeavours (Fiszbein 2000; Jones 2000).

The addition of extra financial, human, technical and other resources from businesses, NGOs and from beneficiaries themselves allow in turn for an expansion in the supply of public goods and services; the expansion of citizen monitoring of public services (Kernaghan 1993: Hawranek 2000); and the creation of new capabilities in the process of establishing and being part of a partnership (Batley 1996: Fiszbein and Lowdon 1999).

The facilitation of creativity and innovation and the combination of inputs from individuals and organisations from different backgrounds and expertise creates a store of specialisation, and hence the ready adoption of new technologies to address issues and problems of society (Edwards and Dearkin 1992; Fosler and Berger 1982; Fiszbein 2000).

In short, much of the 'advocacy' literature on the virtues of public-private partnerships tends to emphasise the complementarities of interests and resources among state, political and private actors. Yet it is very unlikely that all of the above benefits are going to be obtained in practice, and, in fact, many possible drawbacks have already been identified.

In the first place, most of the policy literature on PPPs is derived from the experience of industrialised, high income, Northern countries where the policy was first implemented from the 1980s onwards (Davis 1986; Edwards and Dearkin 1992; Fosler and Berger 1982; Squires 1989; Kernaghan 1993; Batley 1996; Nickson 1995; Hawranek 2000; Jones 2000; Spiering 2000). In this context, state services were already 'going concerns' with near universal coverage. The state had strong institutional capacity and the private sector was mature and large. Hence the creation of PPPs was more in the nature of a transfer, in which cost recovery for the private operators was feasible, and strong regulation at least possible, if not always politically acceptable (Plummer 2002). The contrast with the situation in Southern, especially African, states is obvious; where the problem is more about the extension, or creation from scratch, of services for communities which currently lack them altogether, both in urban and rural areas.

Thus, it would seem unlikely that large scale, technically sophisticated private operators would have much incentive to provide better services to poor communities in the Southern context. Nor would they have much understanding of how to operate in those contexts. Even in a high-income country context, it has been acknowledged that PPPs have tended to widen the gap in service provisions between rich and poor (Devas et al. 2001). The private sector tends to cherry-pick, leaving the state to provide a 'basic' or last resort service for the poor.

It is also clear that regulation and contract management, and hence improved service performance standards, are likely to be problematic, for technical and capacity reasons alone (Batley 1996). The political context of privatisation in a typical African political economy is such that it makes effective regulation in favour of the poor unlikely.

Sustainability is a further problem acknowledged, even in the advocacy literature (Tennyson 1994; USAID 1997; Fiszbein 2000). 'The circumstances under which a partnership is created tend to be idiosyncratic (and hard to predict)...partnerships... are largely episodic outcomes from temporary alliances rather than more enduring arrangements' (Fiszbein 2000: 174). Furthermore, public-private partnerships appear to be vulnerable to changing political circumstances, affecting the survival of the alliances that supported them in the first place (Fosler and Berger 1982; Fiszbein 2000).

One response to these difficulties is to use arrangements which maximise public ownership and control, hence the ability both to set 'social objectives' for the private providers; and capacity to ensure reversion of the service to the public whilst retaining the accumulated benefits of the private investment. This is especially prevalent in the areas of urban sanitation, water and solid waste, where market competition is unlikely to provide services for the poor. For these services, various mixes of contracting out, management contracts and concessions, leasing of assets and even the notion of 'build-operate-transfer' are most frequently used (World Bank 1997; Kerf and Smith 1996; Batley 1996; Walsh 1995; Tennyson 1994; Sinclair 1999; Kernaghan 1993; Stephenson 1991; Pierre 1998).

But even with these kinds of partnerships, the problem of ensuring more comprehensive and improved delivery to poor communities in the urban informal settlements remains, even where decentralisation of the responsible public authorities has been implemented; in fact, decentralisation itself raises worries about increased spatial inequalities (Collins 2000; Fiszbein 1997; Sindane 2000).

Another response to the problems of inequity, 'market failure' and the lack of political sustainability has been to pursue forms of co-production, and strategies, which emphasise partnerships with community-based and beneficiary groups, community businesses and micro-enterprises, termed 'small-scale independent providers' (Plummer 2002).

The problem of co-production strategies in these settings derives from a frequent over-optimism on the part of policymakers about the willingness and capacity of poor communities to provide what are essentially public goods in the absence of public provision. Devas refers to 'residualism': the assumption that when confronted with either the inability or the unwillingness of the public authorities to provide adequate public services, as in the Ghanaian case, deprived local communities, will somehow spontaneously step in to provide funds, labour or organisational support in order to help provide their own services. Thus the 'gap' will be filled (Devas et al 2001: 16).

Underlying this assumption is the familiar, perhaps often romanticised, notion of the social solidarity of the slum, according to which the ethic of caring for neighbours and friends in adversity translates into a strong spirit of collective action on local issues. The most optimistic advocates suggest that partnership action in itself has a feedback effect, strengthening the capacity of civic organisations, and building social trust (Edwards and Dearkin 1992; Fosler and Berger 1982; Fiszbein 2000).

In practice, there are real problems with 'collective action'. As many urban sociologists have long pointed out, urban poverty especially in situations of mass unemployment, housing insecurity and immigration can just as readily lead to social fragmentation, anomie and harsh competition emerging from the struggle of individuals and households for daily survival (Jaglin and Dubresson 1993; Easter 1993; Halfani 1997; Blore 1999). Can the problems of lack of water supply, uncollected solid waste and unsanitary conditions, which make the lives of such urban dwellers so difficult, be solved by an appeal solely to goodwill or public-spiritedness? What makes such social groups transcend individual concerns and take the forms of collective organisation and action, necessary if they are going to make an organised contribution to the provision of these kinds of services? At first glance, the obstacles seem enormous. In the Ghanaian cases, it is clear that political and material incentives played a large role in the community based partnership strategies which emerged.

Case Study of Partnerships and Services in Ghana

In Ghana, citizen-based organisations such as town development committees (TDCs), youth associations and home-town development associations have long existed. They have a long history of cooperation with government in the provision of village and town communal facilities (Badu and Parker 1992; Brown,1990). The TDCs were a formal part of the local government system in the 1960s and 1970s, although the so-called 'unit committees' replaced them after the district assembly reforms of 1989, originally as part of Rawlings' aspiration to create popularly elected 'revolutionary' organs at grassroots level. Given the continuing failure of the unit committees (Crook 1999), the developmental and service provision roles of the TDCs have been continued by citizen-based organisations such as the residents associations, parent-teacher associations, youth associations, town or area development associations, and urban 'home town' associations. The latter tend to be most vigorous and effective in the middle and upper income areas of the cities; or, as in the case of Accra's La Mansaamo Kpee, depend upon the 'patronage' of elite elements and successful sons and daughters who have moved away (Yankson 2000).[2]

Most of the studies of service partnerships between state and non-state actors in Ghana have tended to concentrate on the two main cities, Accra and Kumasi, to the exclusion of the majority of the other local government districts, which, by definition, are more economically deprived. Within these two cities, there has been an emphasis on the technical performance and environmental impact of privatised water supply, or on public-private partnerships in the provision of services like sanitation, education and health. The most detailed work on solid and liquid waste management has been done by Post and his collaborators have done (Yankson 2000; Devas and Korboe 2000; Gough, 1999; Gough and Yankson 2000; Post 1999; Obirih-Opareh and Post 2002; Frantzen and Post 2001).

Some authors, echoing the points made in the general literature on the problems of applying PPP models to low income countries in Africa, have questioned whether decentralised governments in Ghana have the capacity to manage partnerships, in spite of numerous donor-funded capacity-building programmes (Laryea-Adjei 2000; Larbi 1998).

There have been little analysis of the political context within which public-private partnerships have been introduced, hence of the political pressures which have shaped the choice of partners and the effectiveness of performance monitoring. Whittington and others carried out a major survey of popular attitudes to sanitation and the possible cost of sanitary improvements in Kumasi in the early 1990s, concluding that it was unlikely that the mass of the poor households, which were reliant on public toilets, would be willing to pay for anything more than upgrading to KVIP latrines for each dwelling—and even this would require public subsidy.

The introduction of water closets (WCs) with local sewerage would require subsidies so huge as to be regarded politically unfeasible (Whittington et al. 2003). With donor funding, public policy has continued to pay lip-service to the idea that public toilets should be phased out in favour of household-based or dwelling place facilities. But sufficient funding has never been allocated beyond a pilot project.

Conversely, a later study argued that poor households were not sufficiently interested in the 'privacy' benefits of dwelling place facilities to be willing to pay anything; and that the best pro-poor policy would be to provide more and better public toilets. But this has never happened because of the city government's interest in using public toilets as revenue-raising, hence patronage, devices. This has suited the interests of those who benefited from a policy of private franchising of toilet management (King et al. 2001).

Frantzen and Post (2001) also suggest that 'political interference' is behind the failure to-date of public-private partnerships to provide better waste management and sanitation services for the poor in Accra and Kumasi. But they go on to argue that 'community control' of sanitary facilities is perhaps the only way of ensuring greater accountability of service providers to users. The history of public toilet privatisation in Kumasi and Accra suggests that the political power of elected members and city officials, community politics, and the patronage opportunities offered by this form of privatisation are inextricably linked. They cannot be 'de-politicised' least of all at a community level. It is only when these realities are recognised that different and perhaps more effective policies can be developed (Ayee and Crook 2003).

The current New Patriotic Party government came to power in 2001 and attempted in the same year to privatise water as a means of recapitalising the Ghana Water Company, and making water provision effective and efficient. This could not materialise because the potential benefits were 'amorphous', while many interests such as labour unions, managers and professionals, private suppliers and contractors were threatened (Caulfield 2006). The move also resulted in the formation of the Ghana National Coalition Against the Privatization of Water, an effective advocacy body to retain local control over water. The outcome was a mix of institutional arrangements, which included strengthening regulatory mechanisms, facilitating a public-private partnership in the delivery of urban water, allowing for foreign capital and technical expertise, and facilitating community control of delivery in rural areas (Caulfield 2006; Thompson 1999).

Case Studies of Partnerships in Health

Public-private partnerships have not been limited to infrastructure projects or SOEs. They have been used in the health sector in Uganda, Ghana and Tanzania. In 1997, Uganda, for example, launched a PPP in health as a way of extending its health services with the aim of better utilisation of existing private services and facilities through government subsidy, and to improve access and choice. A further move towards partnership is the 'autonomisation' of teaching hospitals in countries such as Ghana, Uganda, Zambia, Kenya, Mauritania and Burundi, which were inefficient and underfunded, to improve efficiency through arms-length' management, increased autonomy through budget and personnel management, pay scales, and the freedom to charge for services. It will also encourage greater reliance by the hospitals on privately sourced income, and allow governments to redirect more of their health budgets toward primary care services (Caulfield 2006). However, the performance of the 'autonomous' hospitals remained 'paper entities' which suggests that where reforms of this kind are conditional on donor funding, governments play the 'aid game' (McPake 1997:174).

Experiences and Dimensions of Decentralisation in the Context of the Public Sector Reform Agenda

Decentralisation has been considered by many as one of the most important strategies in public sector reform. This is because donors and governments in Africa have considered decentralisation to be a strategy that will bring service delivery closer to consumers, improve the responsiveness of the central government to public demands, improve the efficiency and quality of public services, and empower lower units to feel more involved and in control. It is also meant to reduce overload and congestion at the centre, and speed up operational decision-making and implementation by minimising the bottlenecks associated with the over-centralisation of powers and functions at just one or two points in the hierarchy of a public service organisation or ministry. Consequently, decentralisation seeks to increase the operational autonomy of line-managers and agencies, leaving only broad policy guidelines to be worked out at the centre (Smith 1985; Rondinelli 1989).

Definition of Decentralisation

The concept of decentralisation defies a clear-cut definition. Rondinelli (1981) defines decentralisation as the transfer of authority to plan, make decisions and manage public functions from a higher level of government to any individual, organisation or agency at a lower level. To Smith (1985:1), decentralisation means 'reversing the concentration of administration at a single centre and conferring powers on local government'. In this study, decentralisation is considered the opposite of centralisation or concentration, and involves delegation of power or authority from central government to the periphery.

In the study of politics, decentralisation refers to the territorial distribution of power. It is concerned with the extent to which power and authority are dispersed through the geographical hierarchy of the state, and the institutions and processes through which such dispersal occurs. Decentralisation entails the subdivision of the state's territory into smaller areas, and the creation of political and administrative institutions in those areas. Some of the institutions so created may themselves find it necessary to practise further decentralisation (Smith 1985).

Forms of Decentralisation

There are four forms of decentralisation: political, administrative, economic and fiscal.

Political Decentralisation or Devolution

This involves the transfer of specified responsibilities and resources from the central government to local government units, or to a community, usually represented by their own lay or elected officials. A local self-governing authority or government has five important attributes: its locality or smallness; its separate identity or corporate body; competence (responsibility for specific services and the ability to compel compliance); representativeness; and autonomy in a specified area, including resource mobilisation and management.

The relationship between central government and the peripheral institutions is of partnership and cooperation, not of principal-agent or master-servant. Political decentralisation also refers to the opening of a political space in a country to actors in the society and to civil society organisations (CSOs), other than those in power. It represents the notion of political pluralism as distinct from the tendency central governments to monopolise power through the imposition of single parties or military rule. It also includes the creation and/or strengthening of institutions for enhancing vertical decentralisation: the creation and strengthening of institutions of local government; and horizontal decentralisation: creation of institutions for promoting separation of powers and accountability of the executive such as legislative and judicial structures.

Administrative Decentralisation or De-concentration

This refers to the transfer of state responsibilities and resources from the central government ministries and agencies in the nation's capital to its peripheral institutions in the districts within the same administrative system (field administration). In other words, it is an internal form of delegation of responsibilities among officials of the same organisation, and involves the strengthening of field administrative organisations within the public services of a country. The arrangement is administrative in nature. It does not confer discretionary powers on those units, which are not corporate bodies.

Economic Decentralisation

This refers to efforts to open up an economy to competitive forces, as opposed to dominance by state institutions (state capitalism). It would include privatisation, deregulation, and a range of economic reforms. Under economic decentralisation, market-oriented policies are pursued, and the private sector is regarded as an engine of growth.

Fiscal Decentralisation

This process involves the transfer of financial resources from central government to local government units, taking account of the responsibilities allocated to these institutions. The ceding of revenue to local government units by the central government, the mobilisation and management of resources by local government units, and revenue sharing formula, are indicative of fiscal decentralisation.

The Weaknesses of Decentralisation

Although the demand for decentralisation is strong throughout sub-Saharan Africa, there are serious drawbacks that should be considered in designing any decentralisation programme.

First, decentralisation, in practice, runs up against objections at a political level. Indeed, it is felt that decentralisation dislocates the nation, either by encouraging the appetites of certain regions for autonomy, or by encouraging wealthier regions to operate as self-sufficient territories, to the detriment of poorer regions. The issue of guarantees divides supporters and opponents of decentralisation. What guarantees are there that decentralisation will not encourage or endorse separatist or fissiparous tendencies? (Smith 1985; Nzouankeu 1994)

Second, as the wealth of a country is unfairly distributed, decentralisation is likely to accentuate the already precarious imbalance within the state, because there would be a tendency for poor districts to become even poorer. For poor districts and regions, therefore, autonomy would be void of meaning, because they would continue to be dependent on the state. Moreover, decentralisation is not always compatible with planning policies and strategic development projects (Nzouankeu 1994; Prud'homme 1995).

Third, decentralisation can lead to increased waste and squandering of public funds. Common arguments are about the inexperience of locally elected representatives, the fact that they have received little or no training, and that the political ambitions of local politicians will lead them to lending more importance to their electoral preoccupation in preference to the interests of the people. Although there is admittedly an element of truth in certain of these objections, it should not be forgotten that waste is not confined to decentralised units; and that central government is also guilty of waste, often to a greater extent than the decentralised authorities. Moreover, placing decentralised authorities under the ever-watchful eye of central government is not an appropriate way to properly train locally elected representatives for their task. On the contrary, by giving them a sense of responsibility, and by placing them directly within decentralised structures, their training, which must be undertaken rapidly and subsequently intensified, will be beneficial to the management of local affairs (Smith 1985; Mawhood 1993).

Fourthly, decentralisation is not necessarily linked to democracy because the devolution of power may help to augment the dominance of those who, because of wealth or status, are already powerful at the local level:

> ...it is conceivable, even likely in many countries, that power at the local level is more concentrated, more elitist and applied more ruthlessly against the poor than at the centre. As a consequence, therefore, greater decentralization does not necessarily imply greater democracy let alone power to the people — it all depends on the circumstances under which decentralization occurs (Griffin 1981:225).

Fifth, decentralisation might be accompanied by more corruption. If, as is likely, corruption is more widespread at the local level than at the national level, then decentralisation automatically increases the overall level of corruption. This outcome might not be bad in terms of redistribution, because the 'benefits' of decentralised corruption are probably better distributed than the benefits of centralised corruption. But decentralisation would certainly increase costs in terms of allocative efficiency, because it would leads to the supply of services for which levels of kickbacks are higher, rather than those for which there is a demand. It is also costly in terms of production efficiency, because it leads to corruption-avoiding strategies that increase costs, favour ineffective technologies, and waste time (Prud'homme 1995).

Corruption is hard to assess and measure, because there are several reasons why it is likely to be more prevalent at the local than at the national level. For one thing, there are probably more opportunities for corruption at the local level. Local politicians and bureaucrats are likely to be more subjected to pressing demands from local interest groups, whose money and votes count, in matters such as taxation or authorisations. In addition, local officials usually have more discretion than national decision makers. Indeed, it is precisely their discretion that is the major theoretical advantage of decentralisation. The fact that national bureaucrats, at least in some countries, are moved from place to place and never stay very long in the same location makes it more difficult for them to establish unethical relationships with local interest groups, unlike local bureaucrats, whose careers are spent in the same location (Prud'homme 1995).

At the same time, there are fewer obstacles to corruption at the local level. Corruption in many cases requires the cooperation of both politicians and bureaucrats, and the distinction between them is generally less rigorous at a local level. Local bureaucrats have less independence from local politicians than national bureaucrats do from national politicians. In some countries, at least, national bureaucracies have a tradition of honesty that is often absent at the local level. Monitoring and auditing are usually better developed at the national level. The pressure of the media, inasmuch as it exists, would also be a greater disincentive at the national than at the local level (Prud'homme 1995).

Thus decentralisation may not always be a panacea. Its costs are more certain than its benefits. Decentralisation refers to both a state and a process. For both concepts, the virtues and the dangers of decentralisation are often discussed simultaneously. This confusion is dangerous, because what is desirable in a given country at a certain point is a function of the present state of decentralisation and the speed with which it has been reached.

Two Case Studies of Decentralisation in Africa[3]

Ghana and Uganda are commonly cited as the two countries that are examples of relatively good practice decentralisation in Africa. Three of the most important indicators of decentralisation — upward accountability; downward accountability; and combating corruption and the elite capture of the local government units — will be used to assess the state of decentralisation in the two countries.

Ghana began its decentralisation programme under Jerry Rawlings' Provisional National Defence Council (PNDC), which, in 1988, passed the Local Government Law (PNDC Law 207). This decentralisation policy — arguably regarded as the most ambitious effort in Africa — was to 'give power to the people' and bring 'democracy to the doorstep of the people', which was the political philosophy of the government at the time. Indeed, the decentralisation policy of the government may be seen as a translation of its 'populist' notions of participatory democracy into the 'democratic fabric'.

This political objective of decentralisation was also emphasised by the 1992 Constitution in 'Chapter 6, Directives Principles of State Policy'. In this regard, the state is enjoined to 'make democracy a reality by decentralizing the administrative and financial machinery of government to regions and districts and by affording all possible opportunities to the people to participate in decision-making at every level in national life and in government' (Republic of Ghana 1991: 36).

Similarly, the National Decentralization Action Plan (NDAP), published in September 2003, indicates that the specific objectives of decentralisation are to promote popular participation in the decision making process; promote responsive governance at the local level; and enhance efficiency and effectiveness of the entire government machinery, through a process of restructuring of the institutions responsible for service delivery to be closer to and accountable to the people (Ministry of Local Government and Rural Development 2003: 1).

As a result of the great emphasis placed on the political objective of decentralisation, its socio-economic development objectives have been treated as secondary, and relegated to the background. This notwithstanding, there is evidence to suggest that one of the main aims of decentralisation is to promote socio-economic development. Thus, the establishment of the regional coordinating councils and district assemblies to 'enhance the capacity of the public sector to plan, manage and monitor social, spatial and economic development. The district assemblies have become responsible for implementing development programmes and…have thus become the focal points for all development activities at the local level' (Ministry of Local Government and Rural Development 2003: 2).

Consequently, under the decentralisation policy, development become 'a shared responsibility of the government, district assemblies, Civil Society Organization, private sector and communities' (Ministry of Local Government and Rural Development 2003: 2).

Ghana's poverty reduction strategy 2003-2005 reinforces the development objective of decentralisation. Accordingly, it envisages that within a decentralised, democratic environment, the government would aim to create wealth by transforming the nature of the economy to achieve growth, accelerated poverty reduction and the protection of the vulnerable (Republic of Ghana 2003:1). In addition, decentralisation 'represents an opportunity to involve more people and more institutions in the formulation and delivery of development policy for poverty reduction and growth'. It is meant to promote responsive and accountable governance at the local levels that would allow for effective participation, equity in resource allocation, and effective delivery of services, especially for the poor (Republic of Ghana 2003: 135).

The increase in the number of districts 1988-1989 from 65 to110, and in 2004 from 110 to 138, without taking into account their viability, is a classic example of the priority given to the political objective of decentralisation over socio-economic development. Indeed, the creation of districts has become a political, rather than a rational, decision. Government believes that the larger the district assembly, the more difficult it is to sustain democracy and promote effective and efficient delivery of good and services. The result is that government is perceived as a monolithic structure with an inhuman face in the locality. As I have argued elsewhere (Ayee 1990, 1992), there is little evidence to support the argument that smaller units of local government are more efficient and democratic than larger ones. Indeed, research seems to suggest that the size of a local government unit is largely irrelevant to democratic culture and behaviour (Newton 1982).

On the other hand, Uganda started its decentralisation programme in 1993 with the promulgation of the local governments (resistance councils) statute, which redefined the status of local councils. The statute was replaced by the 1997 local government act. The long-term goal of Uganda's decentralisation policy is three-fold: to promote popular participation; to empower local communities to make their own decisions; and to enhance accountability and responsibility of local communities to the level where they would get 'value for money'. These objectives have constituted what is perceived as 'democratic decentralization' (Makara 2000).

The stated aims of Uganda's decentralisation reforms can be summarised thus:

- Transfer power to the people and move further along the path of democratisation, and reduce the workload on remote and under-resourced central officials.

- Promote equitable distribution of resources among and within districts, increase the range and authority of elected officers from village to the national levels, free local managers from central constraints and as a long-term goal, allow them to develop organisational structures tailored to local circumstances.

- Bring political and administrative control over services to the point where they are delivered thereby improving accountability and effectiveness in a system that had hitherto been centralised, non-accountable and corrupt, by establishing a clear link between the payment of taxes and the provision of services they finance.

- Promote through participation people's feelings of ownership over programmes and projects executed in their areas; and improve the capacity of local councils to plan, finance and manage the delivery of services and thus improve public sector performance through enhanced local decision making and political control (Golooba-Mutebi 2004: 289-304).

Upward Accountability

The district assemblies (DAs) have been designated the highest political, administrative, planning, development, , budgeting and rating authorities. Consequently, the DAs have been given eighty-six functions that empower them to provide de-concentrated, delegated and devolved local public services. Specifically, they have been given the power to award contracts not exceeding 250,000,000 cedis. They can also make by-laws, which are subject to approval either by the ministry of local government and rural development (MLGRD), or the regional coordinating council (RCC), before they become operative. In spite of the devolution of authority, DAs are not autonomous. For instance, their exercise of authority is monitored by the RCC, which has the tendency to control their activities. In addition, the president reserves the right of intervention to declare a district assembly to be in default of the public interest, and can transfer the functions of the DA to a person or group of persons. In June 2005, the president revoked the appointment of all sixteen government nominees in two districts respectively, Komenda, Edina, Eguafo Abirem (KEEA) and Dangme West, because of the fear that the president's nominees for the position of district chief executive (DCE) would be rejected by the respective DAs.

Furthermore, the recruitment of staff by DAs is not permitted without the approval of the office of the head of the civil service. The national development planning commission (NDPC) has to approve district plans in accordance with national development goals; while the ministry of finance and economic planning, in consultation with the MLGRD, is authorised to determine the categories of expenditure of the approved budget of a DA that must be met from the district assemblies common fund (DACF). In Botswana, the situation is not much different. According to Sharma (1997: 65), 'policies are determined at the central government level and major decisions for resource allocation are also taken there'.

Similarly, competing forms of decentralisation — devolution to DAs, and de-concentration practised by ministries, departments and agencies (MDAs) — have also reinforced upward accountability. The heads of departments of the metropolitan, municipal and district assemblies respectively still take instructions from their headquarters in Accra, in spite of the passage of the local government

108

service Act 656 in 2003, which stipulates that heads of departments of the 'decentralized government Departments which shall be known as the Departments of the District Assembly are answerable to the District Chief Executive (DCE) through the District Coordinating Director (DCD)'.

Associated with this problem is the apparent conflict between certain decentralised departments or organisations, and the line departments or organisations, namely, education, health, fire, forestry, disaster management and library facilities. The 1992 constitution and parliament created the Ghana education service Act 506 in 1995; the Ghana health service and teaching hospital Act 525 in 1996; the Ghana national fire service Act 537 in 1997; the forestry commission Act 571 in 1997; the Ghana library board Act 327; and the national disaster management organization (NADMO) Act 517. All these services and organisations are listed among the decentralised departments of the DAs under Act 462. The apparent conflict between Act 462 and the enactments referred to above raises issue of both policy and law: whether these services could and should be decentralised. The creation of these services and organisations appears to be a move towards re-centralisation.

An important factor undermining the autonomy of the DAs is that they must deal with several masters or political layers: the president, regional minister, ministers, party officials, the opposition, assembly members, multinational corporations, donors and residents. These are powerful players. Their officials, especially the district chief executives, have become fish of big political pawn, boiling in a political crucible. This confirms the view of Polidano and Hulme 1997: 2) that 'notwithstanding their responsibility to the local electorate, local authorities are often enmeshed in a web of accountability relationships with central government bodies'. It is poignant to note that there is lack of coordination among the various institutions and the local government units, as a result of a lack of appropriate and committed staff, inadequately designed procedures, and inter-ministerial competition.

To ensure balance between local autonomy and central control for the sake of political stability, coordination of development projects and harmony between local and national aspirations, local governance institutions in Uganda must conform to upward accountability. The institutional framework of promoting accountability has been set out as follows (Makara 2000:83):

- The Ministry of Local Government has developed financial and accounting regulations, which local governments must comply with.

- The internal audit department of each local government ensures that all monies are properly spent and reports to the local council and not to the administration.

- The office of auditor-general is established in each district.

- Each local council has a public accounts committee to oversee expenditure and project implementation.

- There is a tender board committee whose members are drawn from the council as well as outside the council, and whose members are not supposed to tender for supply to the council.

- The office of the inspector general of government services receives complaints from anyone who feels that there is proper use of local council resources and investigates.

- Existence of a local government finance commission, which advises the minister and the president on the distribution of revenue between the central government and local governments and among local governments, and on matters of equalisation and conditional grants and other financial matters.

Upward accountability is ensured because district councils and sub-county councils are entirely dependent on transfers from the central government, even though they have power to mobilise resources and use them as they wish. Central transfers are either in the form of conditional grants (CGs), which as, as in the Ghanaian case, driven by national ministry decisions in areas such as primary education, primary health and feeder roads; or they are in the form of unconditional grants (UGs), used for fixed administrative costs. Local taxes contribute between 4 and 9 percent of district revenues (Wunsch and Ottemoeller 2004).

The over-reliance of the councils on conditional grants and unconditional grants from the central government has buried 'local governments in mountains of paper and ever-changing requirements to comply with reporting demands. Much staff time is invested in both the CGs and UGs, but delivers no services to any citizen' (Wunsch and Ottemoeller 2004: 199). In addition, national ministries, rather than councils, largely dictate local plans and budgets. As a result, councils are unable to set and meet local priorities. Accordingly, Wunsch and Ottemoeller (2004: 198) have concluded that 'Uganda has experienced more a move to de-concentration than devolution or democratic decentralization'.

These caveats notwithstanding, the objectives of decentralisation in Uganda, unlike in Ghana, seem to have affected the nature of power of the central government. Unlike in Ghana, the minister of local government has been deprived of most of the powers he previously held before 1993. For example, he has no powers to approve budgets or by-laws of local governments; or to revoke them; or to terminate the mandate of a councillor; or dissolve a local government council. To dissolve a council, the minister can only seek the amendment of a law in parliament; a local council can only be dissolved in times of emergency. However, as in Ghana, the minister must approve any borrowing where the value exceeds 70 per cent of what a local government may legally borrow. The minister must also be satisfied that the previous year's accounts are audited and certified by the auditor-general (Makara 2000; Devas and Grant 2003).

Downward Accountability

The hallmark of decentralisation has been downward accountability. There are elected councils at the village and other levels of local government. The significance of elected councils is two-fold: civil servants, unlike in Ghana, are appointed and paid; and their services may be terminated by the district service commissions, instead of by central government. Civil servants are collectively and individually responsible to an elected leadership of the district. The district service commission deals with grievances of civil servants affected by adverse decisions of persons in higher positions of authority at the local level. As in Ghana's case, the district council is the highest political and legislative body in the district. The chairperson of the district is the political head of the district; but unlike in Ghana he is elected. District councillors are also elected by universal adult suffrage, but at a sub-county level.

As well as elections, local authorities are required to publicly display information about their resources available for local service delivery. This has started to build a degree of public awareness, and demands for greater accountability for resource use. In the process, citizens can question those responsible about use of money (Devas and Grant 2003). In addition, as in the Ghana case, radio stations have ensured downward accountability through organising programmes that feature the chair and councillors in discussion about local governance problems and ordinary people's concerns.

Downward accountability appears however to be weakened by two factors. First, the dominance of conditional grants (CGs), and the parallel planning and budgeting process, that undermine local planning. Secondly, by the ineffectiveness of council committees, at both sub-county and district levels, and the tendency of councils to overbudget: 'This meant local elected representatives lost an opportunity to set priorities and to discipline decision making by administrative personnel. Instead, the real or operating budget was in effect determined by the latter' (Wunsch and Ottemoeller 2004: 206).

Combating Corruption and Elite Capture

In Ghana, decentralisation has been used as a form of patronage. The appointment of district chief executives (DCEs), for instance, is seen as a way of rewarding party favourites. The DAs have been bedevilled with cases of outright embezzlement, improper use of council property and facilities, overpricing, and collusion with those who submit tenders. Other corrupt activities include: the suppression of value books, non-recovery of advances, neglect of stores' regulations, and inadequate expenditure control (Ayee 1999). The problem of corruption has been well captured by Devas and Grant in their Kenyan study:

> ...decision-making in the Kenyan Local Authorities remains non-transparent, with most decisions still being made behind closed doors and a lack of publicly available information on budgets and accounts. There are major problems of corruption, improper accounting, abuse of tender procedures, over-employment of junior staff for political reasons and poor relationships between paid officials and elected councillors. Upward accountability is also weak, due to the limited capacity in the Ministry of Local Government to monitor the activities of Local Authorities or take effective enforcement action. Inspections are often seen as rent-seeking opportunities by those involved (Devas and Grant 2003: 314).

The African Peer Mechanism Review (APRM) Report on Ghana in 2005 also confirmed that corruption indeed exists in decentralised bodies. Participants at the various stakeholders' consultations complained about the high degree of corruption in Ghana's public sphere, at both the national and regional levels. In Ho and Cape Coast, stakeholders generally felt that corruption is rampant in decentralised organs of government, such as the metropolitan, municipal and district assemblies (MMDAs). Participants in Wa generally feel that unless one has contacts in Accra, one will not be attended to (APRM Report 2005: 37).

The causes of corruption are listed below (Ayee 1999b: 2-3):

- Failure to adhere to strict accounting, financial and budgeting principles such as award of contracts without following the approved procedure.

- Failure to submit trial balance returns.

- Over-expenditure on the part of local governance institutions as a result to stick to existing regulations.

- Failure to take corrective actions on the recommendations of the audit service to improve financial management.

- Poor monitoring of performance of local government institutions by the ministry of local government.

- The desire to develop fast or to cheat, induces some acquiescence and leads to lack of thoroughness in overseeing project implementation.

- The inability of governments to act on findings and recommendations of commissions of inquiry into corrupt activities in spite of warnings to deal drastically with them.

- Incompetence on the part of accounting staff of local governance institutions; poor auditing.

A lack of adherence to conflict of interest rule by officials and representatives. Inadequate and unreliable information on the activities and financial transactions of local governance institutions. Sometimes publicly displayed information is often out of date and inaccessible to the majority of the people because of the location of display or the language used.

A lack of interest in local governance issues by civil society organisations. Specifically, the public interest has not also been served by the behaviour of some district chief executives and DA members who engaged in transactions where there were clear conflicts of interest. For instance, some DCEs and DA members, or their 'front' partners, have been known to hold DA contracts even though this is in violation of the Local Government Act 462 in 1993. Consequently, there are no fully transparent and performance-based tendering procedures, in spite of the existence of the district tender board, which is chaired by the DCE.

In addition to corruption, local elites have taken advantage of their power, knowledge and networks to use local government units for their own interest:

> ...in most of the African cases, elite capture of local power structures has been facilitated by the desire of ruling elite to create and sustain power bases in the countryside. Popular perceptions of the local logic of patronage politics reinforce this outcome (Crook 2003:86).

There is no gainsaying the fact that in most African countries, local elites have engaged in corrupt practices, probably because there are more opportunities for corruption at the local level. Elite capture is fuelled by a number of things. First, local elites usually have more discretion than national decision-makers. Secondly, most local officials, unlike their national counterparts, stay for a long time in the same location, making it easier for them to establish unethical relationships with local interest groups. Thirdly, there is a perception that the tradition of honesty is often absent at the local level. Fourthly, monitoring and auditing are usually more developed at a national level than at a local level. Fifthly, the pressure of the media, in as much as it exists, is also a greater disincentive for corrupt practices at a national level.

Similarly, in Uganda, in spite of the stringent reporting demands put in place to ensure the UGs and CGs are not embezzled or misappropriated, there is evidence of corruption among the councils. Makara (2000) and Devas and Grant (2003) have catalogued a number of corrupt activities. They include chief finance officers hampering internal audits of local governments, collusion of internal auditors and sub-county officials, irregular auditing, inflation of tender prices for cement by the tender board, and local purchase orders issued to contractors to carry out work when no contract between contractors and the district authorities had been signed.

Elite capture of power in decision making has been achieved through the village councils (LC1). They are responsible for providing security and adjudicating in all petty and non-capital crimes. They are regarded as the 'people's court' patronised by tenant farmers engaged in disputes with landlords. In spite of its obvious pitfalls such as abuse of power and conflict of interest by the elites, the LC1 system has been lauded, because of its ability to empower local people in their relations with the military, who used to be 'untouchable' (Wunsch and Ottemoeller 2004).

Comparing the Ghana and Uganda Cases

In spite of about two decades of implementing an ambitious and comprehensive decentralisation policy, Ghana still has a highly centralised and top-heavy public administration system. This has been acknowledged by the national decentralisation action plan of 2003. According to this plan, in spite of the constitutional provision that Ghana must decentralise the administrative and financial machinery of government to the regions and districts, the reality has been a growing concentration of power and resources in the key ministries, departments and agencies (MDAs) , which plan, implement, monitor and evaluate essential services to communities (Ministry of Local Government and Rural Development 2003:4).

This point has been re-echoed by the forum of stakeholders, which served as a part of the validation of the African Peer Review Mechanism report on Ghana, in the eastern, Volta, western, central and upper west regions, for the visiting sixteen-member delegation from the South Africa based APRM in April 2005. According to the APRM report (2005:25):

Stakeholders generally agree that decentralization is not working as it should. At various meetings countrywide, they have made it clear to the Country Review Mission (CRM) that real power (be it administrative, financial or political) should be delegated and extended from the centre to the decentralized structures at the regional, metropolitan, municipal and district levels. This would make for more accountable, participatory and transparent political governance, financial management and socio-economic development at those critical, grassroots level. Several stakeholders have expressed their preference for elected District Chief Executives and District Assemblies.

As in Ghana's case, the state of local governance Uganda has faced many difficulties, including political interference; highly centralised development funding; weak committees; planning and budgeting systems that do not work to reflect local needs and priorities, efficiently manage resources and ensure accountability to elected officials (Wunsch and Ottemoeller 2004; Makara 2000; Devas and Grant 2003; Golooba-Mutebi 2004).

Even though local government has transferred resources and some control to the districts, councils are hardly arenas of 'grassroots democracy'. In addition, decentralisation has not been able to 'arrest the deterioration in agricultural services, and…improvements in social services are attributable to increases in central conditional funding rather than the very limited scope which decentralized institutions have provided for local decision making' (Francis and James 2003).

However, these issues notwithstanding, Wunsch and Ottemoeller argue that the Uganda case is an advancement over the Ghana case because:

…elected and civil service personnel have made substantial strides in learning their roles in decentralized governance, a local civil society is forming, people have asserted that decentralization had made them 'free to speak our minds' for the first time, as well as offering some advantages in administrative efficiency and local prioritization.…Through the village (LC1) system, rural Ugandans are exposed to locally meaningful democracy and they have been given an institutional framework for local collective action. At minimum, the LC1 system acts as a training ground for the practice of electoral democracy and an incubator for the notion of autonomy from the state (Wunsch and Ottemoeller 2004:207-208).

115

In addition, the district political head is elected while there are no government nominees in the councils. Furthermore, the sub-district structures are all in place and working, unlike in Ghana, which is still grappling with installing sub-district structures.

Alternative Approaches to Accountability

As the Ghana and Uganda case studies show, accountability is so important to local governance that the search for alternative approaches continues. Accordingly, in spite of the failure of both internal and external mechanisms, it is possible to look to alternative approaches that may be feasible. Alternative approaches involve either a hybrid of the internal and external mechanisms, or the fine-tuning of existing approaches.

Alternative approaches to local level accountability provide citizens with adequate and reliable information, which will build confidence and trust; and de-monopolise service provision by encouraging not only the private sector but also civic participation. Some countries in Africa, such as Ghana, Uganda, Zambia, Tanzania and Uganda, have begun to undertake social service delivery surveys, which identify relevant and useful indicators of service delivery performance, establish a baseline for these indicators, and set targets for future performance. The objective behind community involvement in regulating performance is to increase accountability of service providers, to reorient the provision of services towards citizens' concerns and priorities, and to voice those concerns and priorities. The success of course will depend on the validity of the assumption that community groups are independent of and able to challenge politicians.

They would establish institutions that make key decisions by setting local priorities, allocating resources and supervising the implementation of the decisions. If genuine benefits of privatisation — competition, market discipline, sensitivity to customer satisfaction — are to be obtained, then contracts for the delivery of public services — especially essential services such as sanitation — need to be based on fully transparent and performance based tendering procedures.

They would regulate and monitor contract performance, which must also be independent and rigorous, and the enforcement of conflict of interest laws. They would involve rigorous commitment at top management level, effective systems of performance and resource management audit, and enforcement of due process, combined with an organisational mechanism for making managers take seriously citizen satisfaction surveys and other user measures.

Expanding the financial base of local governance institutions. The financial robustness generated by such autonomy and power has the potential of making the institutions financially self-reliant and reduce their dependence on the central government. This will assist them to carry out programmes based on local needs and oblige them to be accountable to tax payers. Finally, they would promote and encourage an active civil society, a politically conscious or educated population and a democratic political culture on which 'people's power' hinges (Ayee and Crook 2003:1-34).

Decentralisation, Local Government and the Democratic Wave in the Late 1980s and Beyond

Although many African states have pursued substantial decentralisation reforms since the late 1980s, the achievements of many of these reforms have been limited. They are still experiencing problems in bringing about effective local governance. Often, problems stem from the difficulty in translating general reform initiatives into specific working arrangements, at the local level, that are effective in several key processes and operations. Specifically, these include planning and capital investment, budgeting and fiscal management, personnel systems and management and finance and revenue. These four functions are all critical for effective local governance. At the same time they are areas where substantial resources are distributed; and where, given the intense competition for resources generally accepted as typical of contemporary African states, one might expect substantial competition from actors in these states to retain or capture those resources (Wunsch 2001, 2000).

Even though several key organisational arrangements have been used in African states to facilitate decentralisation and structure local governance, none of these have worked particularly well in encouraging the development of genuine local-level authority, the transfer of resources to localities, development of a broadly based process of accountability, or building institutions that work effectively and reliably to facilitate decisions, and make them realities.

A combination of central reluctance to relinquish authority in these key areas and the complexity of organisational redesign to support decentralisation explain these problems. For instance, authority and resources are captured by either central or local actors, or both, who have an interest in preventing them from reaching local government units, and/or because the design of the local institutions and processes is frequently flawed. At times there are operational problems in the four function areas because of the simple difficulty of building working local institutions which can provide complex and technically demanding services in Africa's context of scarcity and general turbulence (Wunsch 2001; Adamolekun 1999; Olowu 1997). As rightly pointed out:

With the exception of Botswana, where a very unusual political environment may have overcome turbulence and allowed a more broadly based political life to exercise some influence over the centre, and whose relative wealth (diamonds) may have temporarily altered the intense competition characteristic of Africa's severe scarcity, a top-down, decentralization/local governance strategy still faces substantial challenges in contemporary Africa (Wunsch 2001: 266-67).

Major explanations for the failure of decentralisation programmes, which have been often described as 'recentralisation' programmes, in Africa can therefore be summarised as:

- Over-centralisation of resources.

- Weakness of central governments (comparative experience shows that decentralised governments function better in countries with strong central governments than in those with weak central governments).

- A mis-match between functions and resources as a result of limited transfers to sub-national governments.

- A weak local revenue base.

- Lack of local planning capacity.

- Limited changes in legislation and regulations; inadequate qualified, underpaid and unmotivated staff; political interference, corruption and abuse of power.

- Weakness of intergovernmental arrangements (especially intergovernmental transfers).

- An absence of meaningful political process; a lack of downward accountability.

- Over-emphasis on fiscal balance at the expense of sustainable community development (Adamolekun 1999; Olowu 1997; Robinson 2007; Conyers 2007).

The failure of decentralisation programmes in Africa may be explained from the perspective of its implicit objectives, which may be called the 'politics' of decentralisation. Because no government is likely to give way willingly, without good reason, one finds that decentralisation programmes inevitably have some ulterior political motives of a centralising nature, in the sense that they are intended to strengthen, rather than weaken, the role of the central government in some way or other.

Decentralisation may be used as an instrument for mobilising support for specific objectives. For example, as a means of increasing support for the government, by increasing 'democracy', or tackling widely recognised social and economic problems, or as a means of avoiding an even greater loss of power, as when a government decentralises in order to meet the demands of a region, which might otherwise breakaway entirely. Moreover, for similar reasons many so-called decentralisation programmes have strong elements of centralisation. This may mean either that the degree of decentralisation is actually very limited, or that the reform involves both decentralisation and centralisation – in other words, that the central government gives with one hand and takes back with the other (Conyers 1989). It has been noted that:

> Anglophone countries have moved faster in implementing decentralization policies faster than the Francophone countries because of the carry over from the former colonial rulers: Britain's decentralized 'indirect rule' system in Africa and the extension of France's centralized national administration to its colonies in Africa (African Development Bank, 2005:159).

'Successful' Cases of Decentralisation

Notwithstanding the negative image of decentralisation in Africa, Olowu and Smoke (1992) identified seven case studies of 'successful' local governments in sub-Saharan Africa, highlighting the principal factors contributing to their success, and exploring ways in which they could further improve their performance. Two case studies came from Zimbabwe (Harare City and Gokwe District councils), Kenya (Karatina Town and Murang'a County councils) and Nigeria (Lagos Municipal council and Onitsha local government) respectively, while one came from Benin (Cotonou Urban District 1).

In these cases, entities were able to raise revenues to provide basic services and generated recurrent budget surpluses. The determinants of success included: location in an area with an adequate economic base; well-defined responsibilities in a satisfactory legal framework; capacity to mobilise sufficient resources; supportive central government activities; and appropriate management practices, including development of productive internal and external relations and satisfactory responsiveness to constituents. Even though these factors were considered necessary, none was independently sufficient to guarantee success, which is regarded as a multi-dimensional process to achievement (Olowu and Smoke 1992).

119

These are no doubt isolated cases of success, which have not been sustained over the years. In addition, the attempt to identify 'determinants of success in African Local Governments' has been regarded as questionable and not very successful:

> Due to the methodological and conceptual problems, the articles suffer from several shortcomings: ambiguous and biased selection of success cases; policy recommendations that are subject to aggregation errors; and insufficiently substantiated generations. The work presented...thus requires refinements along such lines (Therkilsen 1993:505).

Consequently, methodological and conceptual improvements are needed to advance the comparative study of the performance of local governments in Africa. Attention also needs to be paid to equity, resource mobilisation from poor and declining economic bases, and to the impact of political pluralism (Therkilsen 1993).

Apart from the limited and isolated nature of the successful case studies, several scholars have pointed out that in spite of decentralisation in public sector reforms in African countries such as Uganda, Botswana, Côte d'Ivoire, Kenya, Tanzania, Nigeria, Ghana and South Africa since the 1980s and 1990s, there have been 'no real success stories as far as improved development performance at the local level is concerned' (Francis and James 2003; Wunsch 2001; Olowu and Wunsch 2004). This notwithstanding, it is reassuring to note that the:

> ...history of decentralization has not been static. There have been a number of positive changes over the years, including the move to more democratic forms of governance, recognition of the need for fiscal decentralization, and the many recent attempts to increase citizen participation and downward accountability. This in turn suggests that there is a need to see decentralization as part of a long, slow process of state building—and thus to be realistic about what it can be expected to achieve (Conyers 2007: 28).

Strategies for Strengthening Decentralisation and Local Government

A number of strategies have been identified for strengthening decentralisation programmes and local government units. They are as follows (Wunsch 2001; Adamolekun 1999; Olowu 1997; Ayee 1994; Olowu and Wunsch 1995; Rondinelli et al. 1989; Smith 1985; Mawhood 1993; Olowu and Smoke 1992).

A clearly articulate, coherent and comprehensive decentralisation policy, which should be the outcome of consultation between the various economic and political actors/stakeholders in the state, is required. Programmes of devolution (local government) and de-concentration (field administration) must be articulated. Both are necessary and ideally the two reforms should be pursued simultaneously but separately. The articulated policy must define the linkages to the country's programmes of economic and political reforms.

A commitment of the central government's political and administrative leadership to de-emphasise control, transfer adequate resources and appreciate complementarities should be ensured. Adequate powers should be devolved to sub-national levels to ensure that qualified persons are attracted to those levels.

Provide training programmes (especially in institutional development) on decentralisation for not only civil servants but also skill building for personnel at the sub-national level.

The existence of an authoritative responsibility centre for the decentralisation process, which will play the role of coordinating, overseeing and monitoring individual and collective efforts of stakeholders across government and to plan and implement decentralisation-related activities.

For local governance to operate effectively, that is, to deliver locally desired services effectively, to operate internally efficient and to manage social conflict effectively, there must be adequate local authority to initiate and implement policies and programmes; adequate human and fiscal resources to sustain such policies and programmes; existence of a broadly based, informed, attentive and effective local public political life.

Encouragement of decentralisation and the strengthening of local governance should go hand in hand, with each activity reinforcing the other if they are to be truly successful. Significant institutional reform requires the involvement of strong and committed leadership. In the case of decentralisation, this leadership needs to come from both the national government and local communities.

The institution of meaningful reforms in terms of decentralisation, strengthening local governance and enhancement of citizen participation requires considerable time, patience and flexibility. Social and institutional change does not take place rapidly, nor can it be imposed instantly from either outside or above. It also requires recognition that there will be both successes and failures.

Simply changing or amending laws, or creating a local government service does not change behaviour or attitudes. Determined leadership, meaningful technical assistance, sensitisation, training and coaching and experience are also required.

Moving decentralisation forward cannot be brought about without widespread citizen participation and significant efforts to build an inclusive consensus an ownership among the key actors in such events.

Civil Service Reforms: Dimensions and Consequences

Since independence, most policies of African countries towards the civil service and public sector employment have had three common features, each undermining institutional capacity. First, they expanded the size of the public sector faster than the economy grew. Second, they favoured employment growth over income growth in the public sector, driving down the real wages of public sector employees. Third, they favoured pay increases in the lower ranks, reducing pay differences between skilled and unskilled employees. Fourth, many African civil services have been plagued with corruption and other misallocation of resources, ineffective service delivery, sub-minimum-wage compensation, and the recruitment and promotion of unqualified staff (Rasheed and Olowu 1993; Balogun and Mutahaba 1989).

These problems have been difficult to solve because many of the dysfunctional elements help keep authoritarian regimes in power. Bureaucratic budgets reflect the relative powers of bureaucratic elites, rather than the broader public interest. Discretionary import licenses and other economic controls can be targeted to obedient partisans. Patrimonial recruitment and promotion can reward loyalists with jobs, bureaucratic influence, and fringe benefits. Ethnic fragmentation and the lack of the rule of law, transparency and accountability, allows regimes to carry on with the above practices and avoid effective scrutiny and sanction from the broader public (Dia 1993; Easterly et al. 1996). The problems that confronted the Ghanaian and Uganda civil services are summarised below.

Debilitating Features of Ghana's Civil Service Before Reform in 1986

● Substantial overstaffing, especially at junior levels – lack of manpower planning

● determination of real wages/salaries plus a high degree of wage compression

● lack of morale/motivation-incentives problems.

● Inability of major institutions involved in civil service management to provide policy guidance, direction and supervision to sectoral/departmental units – defective managerial competence.

- Over-centralisation and over-concentration of powers and functions at the national level.

- Poor physical work environment and poor facilities — logistical problems.

- Excessive bureaucratisation and red tape e.g., of promotions and appointments to key posts.

- Lack of political direction and commitment leading to apathy and inertia.

- Serious deficiencies in training institutions and programmes.

- Obsolete and rigid rules and regulations resulting from an outdated civil service act.

- Uncontrolled recruitment, particularly in the non-critical occupational grades into the civil service, leading to an undesirable expansion in its size.

- Grossly inadequate low wages and narrow increment differentials, leading to the migration of competent staff to employment zones paying convertible currency.

- Acute understaffing in the senior and professional grades caused by the brain-drain.

- Inadequate legislative framework to support operations and functions of the civil service.

- Declining resources and imbalance between salary and non-wage outlays.

- Questionable security of tenure, anonymity and neutrality (Ayee 2001:4).

Major Civil Service Problems of Uganda Before Reform in 1987

- Dysfunctional civil service organisation.

- Inadequate personnel management and training.

- Insufficient management and supervisory skill.

- Inadequate facilities, assets and maintenance culture.

- Inadequate pay and benefits.

- Inadequate ethics, transparency and accountability, creating incentives for corruption and low staff morale and motivation.

- Underestimation of the required minimum living wage (MLW).

- Distortions in the salary structure.

- Unanticipated negative consequence of decentralisation.

- Other factors: vagueness of CSR policies, leading to multiple interpretations, focus on internal transformational processes (e.g. cost, size, reorganisation). rather than performance criteria (e.g. service delivery).

- Misuse and abuse of office by political and civil service leadership.

- Underestimation of the importance of societal and contextual factors (Langseth 1995).

In short, a narrow, short-term approach to civil service reform is likely to yield limited benefits where governance problems are serious (Dia 1993, 1996). In such settings, recruitment is based on subjective criteria; public employment is part of the social welfare system; pay levels are unrelated to productivity; and loyalty is to the political leader in power rather than to the state. Building a clear public consensus on the need for good governance may be a precondition for creating a more effective civil service. Encouraging professional and other interest groups, allowing freedom of association and expression, and reforming the judicial and legal systems will enable a more productive and responsive public sector and sharply curtail patronage and corruption (World Bank 1995a).

The result is that civil services have become larger than countries need, more costly than they can afford, and less effective and productive than they should be. Reform programmes responded to these problems with short-term cost-containment measures and medium-term programmes to build institutional capacity to increase productivity (World Bank 1995).

Some scholars have stressed the need for a 'top-down', politically-driven, all-encompassing reform process to address such problems. For instance, Werlin (1992: 204), citing the example of countries such as South Korea, argues that reforming central bureaucracies is primarily a problem of political will and government capacity to effectively use persuasive and manipulative (rather than coercive and corrupting) forms of power.

Esman (1991: 138-9), on the other hand, advocates a 'bottom-up' approach. He claims that system-wide reforms disrupt familiar routines and threaten established centres of powers without demonstrating convincingly their effectiveness. He prescribes, instead, incremental, confidence-building measures, such as training, new technologies, for example, micro-computers, introduced with staff participation and focused at the level of individual programmes or organisations. Brautigam (1996) makes a related argument that reforms should concentrate on a few critical functions, shifting politically important patronage opportunities to less vital agencies.

Dimensions of Civil Service Reform

Civil Service Reform (CSR) programmes have increasingly been adopted in Africa, often linked to structural adjustment efforts. The purpose is to improve the effectiveness and performance of the civil service and to ensure its affordability and sustainability over time. The ultimate goal is to raise the quality of public services delivered to the population, and to enhance their capacity to carry out core government functions. This is essential to promote sustained socio-economic development. CSR programmes generally seek to improve both core functions, for example, revenue generation, financial management, personnel management, policy formulation; as well as sector specific policy, management and organisation. Both aspects need to be covered in a coordinated manner (Olowu 1999; Wescott 1999).

The guiding principles on civil service reform were endorsed by the special programme of assistance for Africa (SPA) in November 1995. The SPA is a group of aid agencies that meet to coordinate balance-of-payments and other supports to African countries undergoing economic reform programmes. The principles were developed by drawing on published material, experiences of the donors involved, and six case studies of CSR programmes in Uganda, Tanzania, Ghana, the Central African Republic and Burkina Faso. The case studies were specially commissioned to provide an in-depth assessment of current CSR programmes from a cross section of African countries (Westcott 1999).

The decision by the SPA to recommend broad-based reform efforts rests on a two-part argument: first, African administrations are weak; and second, far-reaching reforms have been successfully carried out by developing countries, both within Africa and in other regions.

The SPA guidelines take into account the top-down and bottom-up approaches. Because of the range of administrative problems, and the political and economic urgency of solving them, African governments need a comprehensive, strategic framework for civil service reform. However, because of the enormity and political sensitivity of the task, and the severe limitations on capacity to manage reform, such a framework will take ten to twenty years to implement fully in most countries.

Implementation needs to proceed in many small stages. Some of these can be planned and scheduled, based on priorities and complementarities. Others will proceed based on targets of opportunity. According to the UNDP (1994) all CSR components need to be developed in a participative way. However, the implementation of some components will require a more direct approach — setting

125

global targets—led by higher-level authorities. Others can be implemented through further consultation and behavioural changes, for instance, ministerial restructuring. Participatory approaches also require donors to adopt flexible project designs that can be changed in response to evolving circumstances. They would usually also require a longer period of preparation.

The guiding principles of civil service reform as adopted by the SPA in 1995 can be summarised as: an overall approach which involves components such as purpose and scope of CSR, economic reform and adjustment, leadership and commitment and taking account of governance; programme design which includes issues relating to diagnosis, vision strategy and preparation, sequencing and timeframe, process approach, strengthening of core functions, ministerial restructuring and decentralisation, downsizing, pay and incentives and capacity building; and implementation, monitoring and evaluation has the components of management of the reform, baseline surveys and service delivery surveys, donor assistance, conditionality, policy dialogue, aid mechanisms, local compensation for CSR management team.

These principles notwithstanding, Olowu (1999:4-7) has noted that even though elements of CSR vary from one African country to another, there are of two broad types: core and non-core elements, which are prominent and consistent. The core elements include organisational restructuring—ministerial reorganisation; creating or strengthening of central coordinating organs; simplification and flexibility; personnel management: improvement of the management of personnel records, retrenchment, ministerial reviews, pay reform; and budgetary and financial reforms which involve three key components, revenue side, expenditure side and systems of financial management and accounting.

The non-core elements, on the other hand, include strengthening the capacity of policy-making institutions, such as the cabinet, as the principal institution for policy making, increasing political responsiveness of top civil servants, and capacity building in the civil service.

Uganda's civil service reform programme introduced in 1990 had a vision articulated by the Public Service Review and Reorganization Commission (PSRRC), which aimed at making the civil service smaller, better paid, more efficient and effective. Fair, simple, consistent rules and procedures were to be implemented to foster discipline while promoting personal initiative. The new Uganda civil service was supposed to comprise workers fully responsible and accountable for their assigned duties and committed to achieving clearly identified individual objectives. In support of this vision, the Ugandan civil service reform programme (CSRP) aimed to achieve sustained macroeconomic stability, improve financial viability in the short- and medium-term, strengthen capacity, and reverse the progressive decline in public efficiency and effectiveness, thereby building public respect and confidence. The design of the CSRP took into account Uganda's changing macroeconomic and institutional context, with emphasis on the government's stated development objectives, decentralisation and army demobilisation programmes (Langseth 1995).

Ugandan Vision of the New Civil Service

The Uganda government set out its vision of the new civil service thus (Government of Uganda 1993).

By the year 2000, the Ugandan Civil Service will be smaller, and it will have better paid, more efficient, and more effective staff. The civil service will have the following characteristics:

- Be result-oriented and transparent.

- Fair and consistent implementation of simple rules and procedures that foster discipline while leaving room for personal initiative.

- Have shared values, supported by regulations that ensure savings and elimination of waste through competitive approaches to purchasing and tendering.

- A new system of resource allocation to local government, based on identified priorities and the unit cost or value added of the services.

- A rational budgeting system based on identified priorities and programmes.

- A mandate to undertake only those functions that it can effectively perform.

- A reduced level of corruption, backed by an effective police and prosecution function.

- Reliable information and databases to support decision making.

- Ugandan civil servants will be paid a minimum living wage; be respected by the public; have clear organisational goals and objectives, and demonstrate commitment to such goals in their work; be fully accountable and responsible for the output of their jobs and committed to achieving clearly identified individual objectives.

Non-core services should either be turned over to the private sector or abandoned altogether. Regulation and control should protect the public interest but also support the expansion of the private sector.

Consequences

The short-term record of civil service reform in Africa is mixed. Most countries have tried to trim excessive public sector wage bills, shed 'surplus' civil service staff, reverse salary erosion, and decompress the wage structure. There has been some progress in reducing public sector wages and salaries as shares of GDP and current expenditure (net of interest). 1985-2002, twenty countries cut their wage bill as a share of GDP, while sixteen increased it. That fifteen of the twenty countries with flexible exchange rates managed to cut their wage bill, while increases were recorded for twelve countries with fixed exchange rates, suggests that real depreciations and the relatively greater wage flexibility in the flexible exchange rate countries were important in reducing the wage bill (UNDP 2001).

Many countries also took steps to reduce the number of surplus civil servants. They used a variety of measures: ensuring attrition through hiring freezes, enforcing mandatory retirement ages, abolishing job guarantees for high school and university graduates, introducing voluntary departure schemes, and making outright dismissals.

Cameroon, Ghana, Guinea, Tanzania and Uganda significantly reduced employment by exorcising payroll 'ghosts' — pay-cheque recipients who did not actually work. The Central African Republic, Congo Brazzaville, Gabon, Ghana, The Gambia, Kenya, Mauritania, Mali, Nigeria and Senegal used various forms of hiring freezes. Guinea and other countries achieved reductions by strictly enforcing retirement-age provisions. And several countries adopted early retirement and voluntary departure schemes — Ghana, the Central African Republic, Guinea, Guinea Bissau, Mali and Senegal. Dismissals were less widely used, primarily in the Central African Republic, Ghana, Guinea and Senegal. Despite these efforts, gross deductions considerably overstate net reductions, because of new hiring (Table 8).

Only a handful of countries have cut the number of civil service employees by more than 5 per cent since they began structural adjustment (Table 9). Moreover, personnel cuts have usually had little fiscal impact, because the cuts disproportionately affected low-paid employees at the bottom of the civil service. Salary erosion has continued, and has frequently been more important in reducing the wage bill than personnel reductions. Although a few countries, notably Guinea, reversed real wage erosion before the period of structural adjustment, this has been the exception rather than the rule. Scattered evidence suggests that the erosion of real wages has been more prevalent in countries with higher inflation.

Few countries in Africa have effective control over the payroll system; in fact, all but six have significant problems (Table 10). To manage the payroll system, governments need to maintain information on who is employed in the public sector and verify this information against the payroll. Personnel censuses can become quickly outdated, unless systems are in place to maintain them and link them to the payroll. Again, governance problems undermine reforms in these areas.

The democratic transition in Africa has also led to reversals of wage containments and personnel reductions in some countries. In Congo Brazzaville the wage bill increased by about 60 per cent in 1991 because of salary increases and a 15 per cent increase in the number of public employees. In Ghana, in 1992 — a year after political transition — wage increases of about 80 per cent compromised the fiscal stability maintained since 1986, casting doubt on the sustainability of the level of public spending. Restoring fiscal balance has proven difficult (UNDP 2001).

Public sector salary spreads have widened substantially in several countries — a desirable development, in that it may facilitate recruitment of talented individuals and provide public employees greater incentives to improve performance. But the data are too limited to establish whether this is a region-wide trend. In Ghana, the ratio of the highest paid echelon to the lowest-paid widened from about 5:2 in 1984 to 10:1 in 2001; and in Mozambique from 2:1 in 1985 to 9:1 in 2001. Salary spreads appear also to have widened in Guinea and The Gambia, though they remained unchanged in the Central African Republic (UNDP 2001). Several countries have devised new administrative structures, redeploying personnel, redefining career streams, adopting formal hiring and promotion procedures and instituting incentive-based compensation systems, using for the most part new public management (NPM) techniques and methods.

In spite of some of the successes of CSR in African countries, scholars such as Olowu (1999) have pointed out that the majority of CSRs have failed because they do not address the serious human resource problems confronting the civil services in the countries concerned. Their diagnosis and prognosis, as well as their strategies of reform implementation, have all been faulty. Specifically, the following reasons account for the failure of CSRs in Africa (Olowu 1999: Langseth 1995; Wescott 1999).

Wrong Diagnosis. For instance, preoccupation with financial costs led to the assumption that the African civil services were too big, while in reality African civil services lacked the numbers and quality of civil servants required to perform policy formulation and management functions.

Sharp Decline in Compensation for Professional Skills. As a result of inflation and currency devaluation, civil servants were forced to do other jobs to supplement their incomes and this has serious implications on effectiveness and efficiency. This invariably leads to a breakdown of the merit system because the civil service recruits people who are unable to find jobs in other sectors like the private, international or civil society and use the civil service job as a last resort.

Weak Systems of Accountability. Because officials who are meagrely paid or irregularly paid cannot enforce ethical codes of the civil service against subordinate officers who are moonlighting or engaging in other illegal activities. In addition, the structures outside the civil service like the Public Accounts Committee and Auditor General Department, which are constitutionally mandated to enforce accountability are weak because lack of critical resources like personnel, office space, equipment, information processing system and library facilities.

Excessive Politicisation and Centralisation. The policy process is dominated by poorly skilled politicians and external consultants. This does not only result in defective policies but also helps to heighten the centralised nature of the civil service.

Wrong Prognosis. The preoccupation is keeping costs down since the civil services were oversized. Thus mandatory personnel reductions/retrenchments became a standard requirement of CSRs. Retrenchment, for instance, has not worked because it is more costly financially than was originally expected and also politically dangerous for governments who fear a political backlash from the labour movements.

Exclusion of Stakeholders. Strategy and fundamental dilemmas that involve the exclusion of major stakeholders, the civil servants, even though their participation would have made the reforms more sustainable. In addition, there has been no nexus between CSRs and other political and economic reforms. For instance, the CSRs in most African countries do not include critical public sector reform issues, such as decentralisation, strengthening accountability and improving transparency — important building blocks in political and economic spheres.

Factors that can Promote Effective Civil Service Reform

Using the Uganda experience of civil service reform, Langseth (1995) has identified ten major factors that will promote sustainable and positive civil service reform in Africa (Langseth 1995:367-369):

- The degree to which the reforms are 'home-grown': The major stakeholders must set the reform agenda. Only if citizens feel involved in, and committed to, the agreed goals will the goals be met and sustained.

- The degree to which the government is willing to take an active part in an innovative and adaptive process: There is the need for African countries to adapt to rapidly changing circumstances, as well as to synthesise and to use existing levels of best practice.

- Strength and sustainability of support from top policy makers: The depth of commitment of a nation's top political leadership is crucial to any lasting success of a new civil service and other initiatives. Bottom-up strategies will succeed only if the will of top political leaders reflect the wishes of their constituents. In other words, the president and his cabinet must actively support reforms that mirror public opinions.

- Extent of consensus about the vision of reform and its implementation: The success of the reforms depends on the extent of consensus not only on the problems, but also on the means of solving them, both in theory and practice.

- Amount of synergy between different reforms: New civil service initiatives are but one in a river of necessary change for effective governance and economic stability. With this understanding, Uganda carried out five reform programmes, namely, civil service reform, decentralization, privatization, constitutional reforms and economic reform. These programmes were coordinated and managed so as to maximum synergy.

- Minimum living wage: Paying civil servants a minimum living wage does not guarantee improved service delivery, but it is a critical (and often neglected) prerequisite for successful civil service reform.

- Service delivery orientation: More emphasis needs to be placed on result-oriented management and the impact of government intervention on service delivery. Both the design and the later monitoring of the impact of the civil service reform on service delivery to the public can benefit significantly from the application of a civil service delivery survey.

- Ability to enhance ethics, accountability and transparency: Lack of accountability, unethical behaviour and corrupt practices have become entrenched and even institutionalised norms of behaviour in the public service sector throughout Africa. Corruption can only be eliminated when both the political leadership and the public makes a concerted effort not to tolerate it. Without a successful enhancement of ethics, accountability and transparency resulting in a curbing of corruption, very few reform efforts in Africa will succeed.

131

- Extent of coordination of donor support: Appropriate and timely support from the donor community is critical to the success and sustainability of the reform.

- Clarity regarding the desired role of the state: Senior policy makers must identify the basic mission and policy objectives of the reform and fully articulate a vision for the state.

Table 8: Reductions of civil service personnel in selected African countries 1990-2000

Country	Removal of 'ghost' employees	Enforced/ early retirement	Voluntary retirement	Regular staff	Temporary staff	Other mechanisms	Total[a]
Cameroon	10,840[b]	10,000	-	-	-	-	20,840
CAR	4,950[b]	-	2,200	700-800	-	-	8,500-8,550
Congo	-	-	-	-	-	4,848[c]	4,848
The Gambia	-	-	-	1919	4,871	-	6,790
Ghana	35,000d	57,235[e]	-	100,375	-	-	192,610
Guinea	2,091[f]	20,236	2,744	-	-	50,793	76,863
Guinea Bissau	1,800[d]	2,945	2,960	2,921	-	-	5,226
Mali	400	-	2,600	-	-	-	3,000
Senegal	1,49[7]	2,747[h]	3,283	-	-	-	7,527
Uganda	20,000[i]	50,000	-	80,000	-	-	150,000

Notes

(a) Gross figures, not adjusted for new recruitment and attrition.
(b) Includes elimination of double payments as well as 'ghosts' (fictitious employees).
(c) Attrition and hiring freeze.
(d) Includes 'ghosts' identified but not necessarily removed.
(e) Includes staff in district assemblies and in the education sector.
(f) Includes 'ghosts' in the Conakry area only. A second census later identified many more 'ghosts'.
(g) Parastatal liquidations and the transfer of joint-venture mining workers to company rolls accounted for 14,983 of these. The remaining officials were assigned to a personnel bank and placed on administrative leave; it is unclear whether all have left the civil service.
(h) An additional 2,133 officials applied for voluntary departure or early retirement.
(i) Estimate based on savings from 'ghost' removal divided by average civil service wages.

Sources: UNDP 2001; World Bank 2000, 2001.

Similarly, Olowu (1999) has identified five major strategies that are crucial in promoting a new genre of African civil service reforms: the re-assertion of meritocracy; improve accountability; decentralisation of operations and structures; mobilisation of resources for civil service reforms; and improvement of information base. It should be pointed out that these strategies are in tune with Langseth's (1995) ten critical factors that will promote sustainable and positive civil service reform programmes in Africa.

Table 9: Change in the number of civil service personnel 1985-2000

Increase of 5% or more	No significant change	Decrease of 5% or more	Information not available
Burundi	Burkina Faso	Central African Rep.	Benin
Cameroon	Chad	The Gambia	Gabon
Congo Brazzaville	Guinea Bissau	Ghana	Madagascar
Cote d'Ivoire	Togo	Guinea	Mozambique
Kenya	Zimbabwe	Mali	Nigeria
Malawi	-	Mauritania	Rwanda
Niger	-	Senegal	-
Tanzania	Sierra Leone	-	-
-	-	Uganda	-
-	-	Zambia	-

Source: UNDP, 2001; World Bank 2000, 2001.

Table 10: Public sector management of the payroll system 1992-2000

Country	Effectiveness
Benin	□□
Burkina Faso	oo
Burundi	oo
Cameroon	••
Central African Republic	••
Chad	••
Congo Brazzaville	••
Cote d'Ivoire	□□
Gabon	••
The Gambia	□□
Ghana	□□
Guinea	••
Guinea Bissau	••
Kenya	⊔⊔
Madagascar	□□

Table 10: Contd.

Country	Effectiveness
Malawi	□□
Mali	oo
Mauritania	oo
Mozambique	••
Niger	••
Nigeria	□□
Rwanda	oo
Senegal	••
Sierra Leone	oo
Tanzania	••
Togo	□□
Uganda	□□
Zambia	□□
Zimbabwe	□□

••   Substantial problems
□□ Some problems
oo   No significant problems

Sources: UNDP 2001; World Bank 2000.

Agencification or Autonomisation

'Agencification', or 'autonomisation', is the practice of new public management to create autonomous or quasi-autonomous public organisations within the public sector. It is a way of building the capacity of the public sector by way of creating a more flexible, performance-oriented civil service. Agencification, which results in the creation of executive agencies, has been adopted in countries such as South Africa, Uganda, Tanzania and Ghana. Its features include: performance improvement, interpreted as quality service delivery to the public; downsizing; increased remuneration of employees; unbundling of traditional departments to create task-specific agencies separate from core departments; agencies created are output-focused, have certain managerial autonomy, are in principle self-financing, and engage in performance contracting with their parent ministries; and they are established by umbrella legislation which gives them statutory basis, although their boards remain purely advisory (Caulfield 2006; Devas et al. 2001).

Agencification has featured in health, and revenue or tax sectors. The most common type of agencification has been the creation of semi-autonomous revenue authorities in some African countries.

134

The semi-autonomous revenue authority as an example of agencification or autonomisation
There has been a big push in Africa for the semi-autonomous revenue authority (ARA) outside the civil service structure, based on the UK executive agency model, for a number of reasons (see Table 11 for some of countries which have the ARA).

Table 11: African countries which have created the ARA

Country	Year of creation
Ghana	1986
Uganda	1991
Zambia	1994
Kenya	1995
South Africa	1996
Tanzania	1996
Rwanda	1998

Source: Devas, Delay and Hubbard 2001: 211-22.

First, the ARA, as a single purpose agency, can focus its efforts on a single task. Second, as an autonomous organisation, it can manage its affairs in a businesslike way or run on business principles, free from political interference and vulnerability in day-to-day operations. Third, freed from the constraints of the civil system, it can recruit, retain, dismiss and motivate staff to a higher level of performance. There is the implicit assumption that such steps would provide incentives for greater job motivation and less corruption. Fourth, it opens up opportunities for more widespread reforms of tax administration. Fifth, it is thought of as one of the most appropriate ways of improving tax administration and collection in developing countries (Jenkins 1994; Silvani and Baer 1997; Devas et al. 2001; Fjeldstad 2003; Taliercio 2003, 2004). Indeed, it has been noted that the driving force behind the establishment of early ARAs in Africa was the

dire financial position of the government and the chronic inefficiency of the existing revenue administration system. Radical action was required if sufficient revenues were to be collected to enable the government to function without at the same time increasing the burdens of the economy. The Revenue Authority model offered a way of starting again, insulating the vital revenue collection function from the rest of the civil service and developing an efficient and effective organization (Devas et al. 2001:213).

In practice, in Africa, the creation of ARAs in Uganda, Tanzania and Zambia has led to increased levels of revenue collections and administrative efficiency, and greater compliance from formal sector taxpayers. However, the ratio of revenue collected by the three ARAs to GDP is not encouraging.

The case for the ARA then is not yet clear. First, it is not even clear what is meant by 'autonomous', because of its multi-dimensional nature. As rightly pointed out by Taliercio (2003: 48-9) there are 'many ways that an agency can be made more autonomous...one agency might have more financial autonomy while another might have greater autonomy with respect to corporate governance'. Similarly, there is a cause-effect relationship in the multi-dimensional nature of an organisation's autonomy, as for example, 'greater autonomy, in addition to providing greater control over the use of resources, has the effect of increasing autonomy over personnel management' (Taliercio Jnr. 2003: 48).

Clearly, the advocates are combining a notion of managerial and bureaucratic autonomy with some concept of political autonomy. But one cannot easily judge whether and how far an authority is autonomous. We know from the South African case, that real success went with a close political relationship between the South African Revenue Service (SARS) and the finance ministry (Smith 2003). Secondly:

the creation of a 'proclaimed autonomous revenue authority with comparatively generous remuneration packages and substantial budgets does not protect the authority from political interference. To the contrary, as observed in the Uganda, it may make it more attractive target because the authority offers both relatively well paid jobs and considerable rent-seeking opportunities. Consequently, such an authority is vulnerable to political interference, especially in personnel matters (Fjeldstad 2003:172-3).

The Efficiency Record of the ARAs of Uganda, Tanzania and Zambia

The total revenue of Uganda rose from 7 per cent of GDP in the early 1990s to 12 per cent by 1999, a success that coincided with the establishment of the Ugandan Revenue Authority (URA) in 1991. However, the ratio has remained stagnant since 1995, suggesting that overall revenue performance has reached a plateau below the level needed to achieve fiscal sustainability. Since 1996, the URA has become increasingly vulnerable to political interference, and public criticism of the revenue agency by high-level political figures has undermined the credibility of the tax administration.

In Zambia the ratio of tax to GDP improved from 17.5 per cent to 18.5 per cent after the creation of the Zambia Revenue Authority (ARA). In Tanzania tax income increased from 11 per cent of GDP 1995-1996, to 12 per cent the year after, but the ration later dropped to 10 per cent, suggesting that the effects of the ARA may be short-lived (van de Walle, Ball and Ramachndran 2003: 85-6).

Continuity and Change in Civil Service Ethos, *Esprit de Corps* and Professionalism

Cutting across the range of skills and knowledge needed to build effective management is the concept of professionalism. Since 1996, conferences and publications on public service professionalism, and the related concept of public sector ethics, have become legion. Much of the current interest has focused on the fight against corruption. Concern over the decline of standards and corresponding need for integrity in public life has driven the debate about the scope and significance of public service professionalism (United Nations 2001).

Professionalism in the civil service is observable not only through relevant and deep knowledge, aptitudes and skills, but also through a coherent, widely shared and profoundly internalised value system, which manifests itself in the thorough pursuit and application of knowledge, the use of particular skills, and the exercise of control over practice. Indeed, it may be argued that professionalism consists in standards and values, which underpin the day-to-day practices and conduct of the civil service. Although these values and standards must, to some extent, reflect the changing expectations of the clients and recipients of its services, they also represent the civil service's own aspirations and deep sense of mission. Hence self-worth is an important guide and motivational tool.

The civil service deals with inter alia the execution of the government's business. It can therefore never be free from the endeavour to promote the ethical conduct of public officials. Three ethical ideals form an integral part of the civil service. They are: a higher form of society, meaning that through the civil service happiness should be brought to society; service to the society, which implies that the civil official's actions should not harm society; and the happiness and well-being of the worker, whereby specific legal or other prescriptions are introduced to safeguard the worker against unlawful or unethical conduct.

Civil Service Ethos

The success or the achievement of the objectives of the civil service depends, in part, on the resourcefulness, commitment, dedication and loyalty of its workforce. There are, however, criticisms about the attitude of civil servants in Africa, which include malingering, apathy, laziness, client insensitivity, abuse of power, misuse of good resources and absenteeism. These negative tendencies have affected job performance, contributing to inefficiency and low productivity.

Other issues that constrain civil services in Africa are inappropriate work habits, corruption and lack of appreciation of time. African countries have realised that if their countries are to achieve developmental goals, become more competitive and attract the necessary foreign investment, then there is a need to reorient the civil service workforce and inculcate it with new work ethics and values. Thus, in line with government commitment to a professional civil service, work ethics based on the following values have been emphasised: competence, dedication, integrity, objectivity, political impartiality, and selection and promotion on merit.

This commitment by African leaders has led to the promulgation of a code of conduct for the civil services. The code emphasised issues relating to the following duties: to be accountable, transparent and customer and client sensitive; to comply with rules and regulations; to give honest and impartial advice to ministers; to ensure proper control of public money; to be courteous to the public; and to maintain confidentialities (Dodoo 1998; Ayee 1997b).

In addition, the constitutions of countries such as Ghana, Uganda and Tanzania have created specialised bodies engaged in promoting a culture of good governance. This is to ensure openness and responsibility in the legitimate exercise of power and power, to manage the affairs of the country in the interest of all the people, and ensure the people's accessibility to the entire civil service. In other words, openness is emphasised in the conduct of public affairs, such that everyone is conversant with the ground rules upon which the system is operating; and civil servants are also required to account for their stewardship to the public. The specialised bodies include the ombudsman institution, media commission, commission on civil education, which can investigate the professional conduct of civil servants and recommend sanctions.

In furtherance of the promotion of good values and ethics in the civil service, some countries such as Ghana have a separate of code of conduct for the service. For instance, in Ghana, a code of conduct was published in 1998. This is in pursuance of Section 92 (3) and (4) (a), of the Civil Service Law (PNDC Law 327) by the Head of the Civil Service, in consultation with the Civil Service Council/ Public Services Commission as part of the administration instructions.

Anti-Corruption[4]

One of the key aspects of public sector reforms in Africa is dealing with corruption; a widely acknowledged index of weak accountability and lack of transparency, in the sense of abuse of public office for private gain. We have seen the incidence of corruption in Africa reach cancerous proportions. In fact, so pervasive is this phenomenon in the region, that it has been labelled the 'AIDS of democracy, which is destroying the future of many societies in the region. The corruption problem in Africa reflects the more general, and now legendary, climate of unethical leadership and bad governance found throughout most of the continent' (Hope 2003: 17).

Corruption has been identified as the root cause of the failure of public management. Some of the causes of public management failure include: poor quality services; inability to make and implement policy or even take routine decisions; weak financial management including unrealistic budgeting and poor control; the practice of employing public resources in the pursuit of private interests, which can be a function of the failure to separate clearly what is public from what is private; the arbitrary application of laws and rules; an excess of rules and regulations which stifle entrepreneurial activity and encourage certain forms of corruption; closed, or non-transparent, decision-making systems; and the allocation of resources which is not consistent with development.

According to Transparency International, these debilitating features enable corruption to undermine good government; fundamentally distort public policy; lead to misallocation of resources; harm private sector development and particularly hurt the poor. In Africa, governments have acknowledged that unless the scourge of corruption is combated effectively, poverty will deepen, the legitimacy of the government will be eroded, human rights abuses will intensify, and democracy will be undermined. Consequently, governments have established institutions to fight corruption. In Ghana, for instance, the government has established the following institutions: Economic Crime Unit of the Ghana Police Service; Serious Fraud Office; Bureau of National Investigations; and the Commission on Human Rights and Administrative Justice.

In addition to the establishment of institutions, leaders have, at least in their speeches, indicated their intention to deal with the problem of corruption. In certain cases, they have punished the 'big fish'. For instance, in 2001, in a gesture to deal with corruption, the government of Kufuor's New Patriotic Party (NPP) in Ghana prosecuted the minister for youth and sports for allegedly stealing US$46,000, being the winning bonuses of the senior national team. Furthermore, a number of ministers and other officials of the Rawlings government were sentenced to prison terms for acts intended to 'cause financial loss to the state'.

Governments have also prepared an anti-corruption action plan. They have acknowledged that several anti-corruption campaigns in the past has failed;

and that new methodologies for fighting corruption involve the building of coalition between government, private sector and civil society; networking; and collaboration from regional and international bodies with support from development partners.

Some countries such as Ghana, Uganda and Nigeria have surveyed the level of perception of corruption. These surveys were regarded as part of a new integrated strategy to fight corruption in the year 2000 and were sponsored by the World Bank. The approach is preventative: to attack the root causes of corruption and fight it with a coalition of internal forces. The surveys provided a firm empirical basis for developing an action plan, the sharing of information and responsibility among partners, and, finally, implementing and monitoring an integrated national anti-corruption programme.

Controlling or combating corruption in Africa is one of the main preoccupations of good governance. Governance principles of accountability, accessibility and availability of information, a legal framework for development, insistence on transparency, freedom of association and participation, and cooperation between government and civil society organisations should be incorporated into a national system of integrity in Africa that can fight corruption. In Hong Kong, where governance features have been incorporated into a national integrity system since the early 1990s, there has been considerable diminution in the level of corruption (Doig 1995).

A drastic reduction of tolerance for corruption worldwide in the 1990s, especially because of its negative consequences for economic growth, is also noticeable in Africa, where many countries have launched anti-corruption programmes, for example in Egypt, Tunisia, Ghana, Tanzania, South Africa, Benin, Mali, Senegal and Uganda. Predictably, anti-corruption measures being implemented include strengthening the enforcement of accountability, and improving transparency and openness in the conduct of government business. Performance targets and monitoring systems have also been instituted. To be effective, results-oriented public sector management has been advocated to create incentive structures and an enabling environment to encourage the achievement of public service reform targets and quality results. These measures notwithstanding, efforts to combat corruption have not been very successful because of the inconclusive nature of measuring the level of corruption (Stapenhurst and Langseth 1997).

Measures to fight corruption in Africa have been set out as follows: committed political leadership that shows its commitment by willingly submitting to a comprehensive monitoring of assets, incomes, liabilities and life-styles; participation by public service unions and other employee's groups; involvement of professional groups as well as community and religious leaders; public involvement and participation in the reform process, with proposed changes debated widely to generate a sense of ownership among the public and reinforce the values embodied in reform; the establishment of 'watch-dog' agencies; improved procurement procedures such as procurement requirements, rules, and decision-making criteria should be readily accessible to all potential suppliers/contractors and procedures should be systematic and dependable, and records maintained that can explain and justify all decisions and actions; de-politicisation of the allocation system and rendering it efficient; refining the resource allocation process itself by, among other things, endowing it with verifiable efficiency promotion criteria; open competitive bidding in the award of major construction contracts and in the procurement of goods and services; buttressing the institutional management with an effective treasury system, a strong auditing system; and public awareness of the role of civil society (Stapenhurst and Langseth 1997: 311-30).

Enhancing Public Service Accountability

In most African states, the abuse of human rights and discretionary power by both politicians and administrators is not only rampant and legion, but also on the rise. This abuse is mostly the result of the complexity and diversity of the state in developing countries, which has increased the power available to governments to pursue socio-economic development programmes. The state in African countries is expected not only to perform the traditional functions of government, such as maintaining law and order, but also to provide education and social welfare, manage health programmes, operate transportation and communication facilities, and organise various cultural and recreational events. Through the performance of these several and multifarious roles, politicians and public servants have acquired enormous power: 'the more society is administered, the more power is concentrated in the hands of politicians and public servants' (Dwivedi 1985: 61).

The exercise of power and authority by politicians and public servants has led to the growth of unethical activities in the public sector in African countries. Politicians become corrupt; citizens are incarcerated in the name of the supreme interest of national security, without the due process of the law; while employees are dismissed without resort to established procedures of labour laws. The more the cases relating to the misuse of power and authority are brought to public attention, the more worried the public becomes. The public in most African states views the state as too big and too powerful, with tendencies of the

141

legendary leviathan. Consequently, there is a demand for a clean administration and improved moral fibre in public officials and politicians, responsible use of power and authority, and administrative accountability (Ayee 1989). The major concern in most African states is how to ensure that those who have power exercise it responsibly, so that they can be held accountable for their actions.

In order to maintain and promote responsible administrative conduct, therefore, it is essential that a means be found to guard against abuse of this immense administrative discretion. Also, there is the need for the creation of an inexpensive, speedy, largely informal and socially effective mechanism whereby the individual can ventilate his legitimate grievances resulting from official maladministration. Without proper democratic controls, the concentration of power in the administration might not only give rise to venality, inefficiency and mistrust of the government, but also increase the risk of subverting the government itself. The quest for a solution to the problem has led to a global search, and to resorting to the institution of the ombudsman, to control at least the incidence of abuse of power (Ayee 1994a).

The institution of the ombudsman's office has spread to African countries as an instrument for enforcing accountability. Whether established by a constitution or legislation, the ombudsman serves as the 'citizen's defender'. The ombudsman receives complaints from citizens, investigates them, and makes recommendations on how they can be redressed at no cost to the citizens. The number of ombudsmen in Africa increased from six to twelve between 1990 and 1996. Countries that had ombudsmen in the pre-1990 period include Tanzania, Ghana, Zambia, Nigeria, Sudan and Zimbabwe. Those with ombudsmen in the post-1990 period include South Africa, Malawi, Mali, Senegal and Namibia (Adamolekun 1999).

Even though the performance of the ombudsman differs from country to country, the very existence of the institution is an affirmation of a commitment to assisting citizens who seek redress against mal-administration. It sends a message to public officials for the need to treat citizens with fairness and impartiality. This notwithstanding, there are certain problems which undermine the smooth operation of the ombudsman in countries that have created such institutions. The problems include lack of adequate resources, the denial of independence, and the tendency to 'bureaucratise' them (Olowu 1999).

Conclusion

This chapter has examined the strategies aimed at improving the efficiency and effectiveness of the public service. Strategies such as privatisation, commercialisation, decentralisation, public-private partnerships, civil service reforms, anti-corruption and agencification have had varying degrees of success in the various African countries. It is clear that even though the strategies or measures have not been as successful as one would have expected, they have permanently placed the issue of public sector reform on the agenda of governments and development partners. Indeed, they have become the building blocks and the flagship of reform in African countries, which cannot be ignored in discussions about the reform of the public sector.

Chapter 6

The Future of the African Public Sector: Alternative Approaches to Renewal and Reconstruction

Introduction

Most observers of African public administration agree that the African public service, especially the civil services, local governments and field administrations were at their best in the years just before and shortly after independence. The hope of the present reforms is to at least revert back to these 'golden days'. As this study has shown, it is clear, thus far, that most of the strategies pursued by African states to reform their public services have not able to achieve the desired outcomes because of political, historical, economic, institutional, cultural and other environmental constraints. The characterisation of the 1980s as the 'lost decade' and of the 1990s as a 'mixed bag at best' gives the measure of the distance between expectations and outcomes of reform efforts in Africa. The task of this final chapter is to identify possible alternative approaches to promoting and enhancing the renewal and reconstruction of the African public sector.

The New Partnership for Africa's Development

Public sector issues have engaged the attention of the New Partnership for Africa's Development (NEPAD) initiative, launched in October 2001 as a blueprint for Africa's regeneration, and previously known as the New African Initiative (NAI). It is the consolidation of two proposals — the Millennium Partnership for the African Recovery Programme (MAP), which had its driving force in presidents Mbeki of South Africa, Bouteflika of Algeria and Obasanjo of Nigeria; and the OMEGA Plan for Africa, which was conceived and sponsored by President Wade of Senegal.

The preconditions for Africa's renewal are captured in the following set of five core principles (Hope 2002; Elbadawi and Gelb 2003).

Good Governance

Proper adherence to good corporate, economic and political governance. Growth and development cannot be achieved in the absence of good governance. Any effort to reduce poverty must start with and build upon good governance.

Entrenchment of Democracy, Peace and Security

Peace, democracy and security are a necessary precondition for attracting investment, garnering growth and development and reducing poverty.

Sound Economic Policy-making and Implementation

This entails the restoration and maintenance of macroeconomic stability, especially by developing appropriate standards and targets for fiscal and monetary policies, and introducing appropriate institutional frameworks to achieve these standards. In addition, African countries should reduce their dependence on foreign aid and seize the historic opportunity that has presented itself to end the scourge of underdevelopment that afflicts the continent, given that resources (including capital, technology, and human skills), that are required to launch a war on poverty and underdevelopment, exist in abundance.

Productive Partnerships

This entails the development of a more productive partnership between Africa and its bilateral and multilateral partners. The overall objective is to improve effectiveness in development cooperation primarily through better practice in the aid relationship, delivery, and reporting systems. This new and better practice would set out mutually agreed performance targets and standards for both donor and recipient countries.

Domestic Ownership and Leadership

No initiative for Africa's development, however, well crafted and internationally accepted, can and will be successful, if it is not owned by Africans themselves. Ownership matters because it directly affects programme acceptance and implementation at the national and local levels. Domestic ownership generates political support and buy-ins by relevant stakeholders who are much more likely to view the initiative as a worthy indigenous one rather than immediately dismissing it as a foreign imposition.

NEPAD is innovative for two reasons. First, in the use of the African Peer Review Mechanism (APRM) to encourage collective action, and promote standards, whether of governance, accountability, or sound economic management. Participating countries enter into a series of commitments to create or consolidate basic governance processes and practices; while a forum operating at the level of heads of state will serve as a mechanism through which the leadership will monitor and assess progress. Second is its emphasis on facilitating, at the political level, regional and sub-regional approaches toward the provision of essential regional public goods, as well as the promotion of intra-African trade and investments. African countries are small and interdependent. Collective action is needed to address impediments to full economic cooperation (Elbadawi and Gelb 2003).

In spite of its potential, NEPAD faces some challenges. For instance, the need for more discussion and internalisation within Africa. So far, formulating and developing the initiative has been a largely top-down process (Elbadawi and Gelb 2003).

Millennium Development Goals

The public sector in African states is expected to work towards the same ends and achievement of the eight Millennium Development Goals (MDGs), which started in 1990 and will end in 2015. The goals are: (i) eradicate extreme poverty and hunger by halving the proportion of people living on less than one dollar a day and the proportion of people who suffer from hunger; (ii) achieve universal primary education by ensuring that boys and girls alike complete primary school; (iii) promote gender equality and empower women through the elimination of gender disparity at all levels of education; (iv) reduce child mortality by two-thirds the under-five mortality rate; (v) improve maternal health through a reduction by three-quarters the maternal mortality ratio; (vi) combat HIV/Aids, malaria and other diseases; (vii) ensure environmental sustainability by integrating sustainable development into country policies, restore degraded environment resources and halve the proportion of people without access to potable water; (viii) develop a global partnership for development by raising official development assistance and expand market access (World Bank 1990).

All countries on the continent are focused on the achievement of these goals. The public sector is faced with a Herculean task, since it is spearheading the implementation of various strategies and initiatives aimed at the realisation of the MDGs.

Effective Local Community Governance

The international community has recognised the importance of effective community governance as a *sine qua non* for development. Local institutions, community based organisations, and other civil society organisations are seen as constituting the nucleus of participation and accountability. In most African countries therefore, public sector reform will continue to be preoccupied with designing effective local governance institutions. This will focus on two broad issues: the process of the feasibility of transfer of authority, resources and accountability, and the development of an open local political process and local political and administrative institutions, which will suggest that local priorities and needs are driving local decision making; and outcomes and outputs: whether local community governance is bringing expected tangible benefits in terms of better schools, health systems, water supply, or roads, or intangible 'empowerment' and social service delivery that enhance people's welfare – intangible outcomes (Olowu and Wunsch 2004).

Redefinition of the Role of the State in Development

As a result of the criticisms of new public management and concerns about social cohesion, equity and stability, interest has been revived in the role of the state in some aspects of development. The debate now is about how to revitalise the state, to enable it to perform its role effectively. As rightly pointed out by the UK's Secretary of State for International Development, the main focus of development policy, the elimination of poverty, can only be achieved 'through strong and effective states'. 'The era of complete enmity to the public sector in general and to state provision in particular is coming to an end' (Minogue et al. 1997).

In the 1997 *World Development Report. The State in a Changing World*, prominence is given to refocusing on the 'effective state'. This marks a significant shift in thinking about the state and its role in development: the need to factor the state back into development. The World Bank has recognised, somewhat belatedly, that reforming the public sector the NPM way does not lend itself to clear, unambiguous solutions. NPM is not a panacea for all problems in the public sector. In addition, there is recognition that the imposition of one template of

147

reform for all, irrespective of the context, is counterproductive, and may even breed conflict and undermine stability. The way forward is to make the state work better, not to dismantle it. Consequently, the World Bank (1997) has suggested two strategies.

The first strategy is to match the role of the state with its actual capability; the earlier mistake being that the state tried to do too much with few resources and limited capacity. The second strategy is to strengthen the capability of the state, by reinvigorating public administration institutions to enable them to perform their enabling, regulating, monitoring and coordinating roles. This will entail creating effective rules and restraints, encouraging greater competition in service provision, applying measures to monitor performance gains, and achieving a more responsive mix of central and local governance, by steering policies in the direction of greater decentralisation (World Bank 1997; Batley 1994).

Reforms Must Be Home-Grown, and Made to Fit Real Needs

Past approaches and strategies at reforms of the public service in Africa took a somewhat dogmatic and technocratic approach, which failed to take account of the complexities of particular national circumstances, and over-emphasised single facets of reform, for example, cutback management, over all others. Criticised as 'reductionist', this approach took for granted a measure of convergence of managerial cultures which appears, in retrospect, as somewhat unrealistic. It correspondingly pressed for 'one best way' solutions, which earned it the description: 'one-size-fits-all'. Instead, customised approaches are required to meet the diverse needs of individual countries. In fact, as rightly pointed out, 'an overly technocratic or purely economic growth approach to institutional development divorces the institutional strategy from the socio-economic strategy and political environment which it is meant to serve' (UN 2001).

A related criticism has faulted the relationship between recipient and donor. Contrary to officially accepted doctrine, too many programmes proved to have been supply-driven. In many cases, accordingly, reforms have been externally induced. Too often, as a result, style has invaded substance, and programmes were concerned with 'quick fixes' rather than long-term progress (UN 2001).

The lessons of experience in Africa strongly point to the conclusion that for reforms to be successful and, accordingly, aid programmes to produce 'user-friendly' results, they must clearly be: home-grown; demand-driven; internally consistent; and duly coordinated at a national policy level.

It has become apparent that the design and conduct of reform programmes require the steady involvement of competent national teams, which must be in the driving seat. Main policy decisions cannot be 'outsourced' to consultants, however good. However, well-intentioned and technically accomplished, foreign advice must stay within the bounds of counselling and guidance. Overstepping that limit is both counterproductive and dangerously short-sighted. Taken too far, it undermines the confidence of peoples in their respective governments and institutions. Democracy is 'hollowed-out', and accountability is lost, when citizens conclu- de that their elected government has lost control of events (UN 2001).

Developing a Public Sector Ethos in Africa

Regional norms for the public service are being put together by the African Training and Research Centre in Administration (CAFRAD) based in Tangier, Morocco. These norms are intended to create a working culture based on quality, performance, openness and transparency, necessarily involving employees and the public in the change process. They are aimed at developing an organisational culture, which manifests itself in strengthened employee involvement, consistency in the change process, rewards for team-work and individual perception, and consultation with clients and users. This formal development of regional norms marks a significant step in moves towards codifying public sector values at a time of rapid change within the culture and practice of the public sector. The norms are expected to professionalise the public sector, and set standards, which will promote efficiency and effectiveness.

Related to professionalisation is human resources development. Almost any document on the public service in Africa indicates that it suffers from acute human resources in critical areas of expertise and skills. It need not therefore be overemphasised that, without a clear policy to address this, the expertise, skills and managerial know-how, needed to make the public service productive and efficient, will simply elude it, and thus render reform expectations barren (Ayee 2001a).

In short, the regional norms being formulated by CAFRAD are part of a wide-ranging campaign against unethical behaviour in Africa's public sector. They also reinforce the following core public values: revaluation of learning, integrity and competence; stress on the merit system, whilst paying due regard to affirmative action in favour of minorities and historically otherwise disadvantaged groups; growing sensitivity towards and respect for citizens' needs; low tolerance for laxity, corruption and crime; increasing recognition of the need to acknowledge and to reward industry, loyalty, accomplishment and merit; increasing recognition of the value of neutrality of civil servants, and of the need to

149

secure a degree of autonomy of public personnel management from extraneous pressures in order to safeguard high quality performance; motivation, integrity and professionalism; and increasing recognition of the value of cross-cultural and international links as means towards the improvement of the professional image and performance of the public service.

Assisting African Countries with Institution-Building

Core public service values can neither be established, nor fostered overnight, without regard for the political, social and cultural environment in which a public service operates, and the appropriate structures and legislative policy frameworks designed to tap, attract, retain, develop and motivate much needed men and women to use their skills productively and effectively. Assisting African countries in building or refining these structures and policy frameworks represents an urgent priority.

It cannot be overstressed that policy advice and programmatic assistance offered by either the bilateral or multilateral programmes must respect the distinctive legal and political traditions of different countries, which vary widely. Some countries adhere to a tenure career system; while others, by contrast, prefer more flexible staffing arrangements. One size does not fit all. Nevertheless, experience strongly suggests the need to professionalise human resources management and development in the pubic service sector (United Nations 2001).

Conclusion

From the range of important initiatives outlined above, there can be no doubt that building better public sector management in Africa is not only arduous, but also time-consuming. Success will depend on commitment, from both politicians and bureaucrats, to economic growth, investment and international competitiveness; rather than focusing on the consumption and waste of public resources. This requires corruption to be minimised; that reforms are made credible and irreversible, and are basically oriented towards equality, and backed by adequate administrative and institutional capacity and sufficient mobilisation of support and of resources for the growth strategy.

Finally, policy learning is a prerequisite. Debates, dialogues, learning by reform failures, learning by analysing policy outcomes, by discussing the causes of weak policy performance, and asking how to cope with the emerging issues in the future may be important steps in this direction. Policy learning also means informing the people and interest groups via civil society organisations (CSOs),

informing people and actors at all levels of the state about governmental policies, and organising a dialogue and a permanent forum between government,
interest groups and CSOs, so that new policies can be truly rooted in African
countries.

Notes

Chapter 1

1. The 2005 African Development Report on Public Sector Management in Africa published by the African Development Bank indicates that the 'public sector' and the 'state' are used synonymously because there cannot be a strong state without an efficient public sector.
2. For an extensive discussion of the 'dead hand' of bureaucracy see G.E. Caiden, ed., 'Symposium on Public Policy and Administrative Reform', *Policy Studies Journal*, Vol. 4, No. 8, Special Issue 4, 1980-81; Peter Self, 'What's Gone Wrong with Public Administration', *Public Administration and Development*, Vol. 6, No. 4, 1986, pp. 329-338; Peter Drucker, 'The Deadly Sins in Public Administration', *Public Administration Review*, Vol. 40, No. 1, March-April, 1980, pp. 103-106.

Chapter 3

1. This chapter draws heavily on Ayee, J.R.A., 'Public Sector Management in Africa', *African Development Bank Economic Research Working Paper*, Vol. 82, November 2005, pp. 1-56.

Chapter 4

1. The three phases are sometimes referred to as 'First-generation reforms', 'Second-generation reforms' and 'Third-generation reforms'.
2. *See:* Crook, R., 2004, 'The State of the State in Africa: What is to be Done?', Inaugural Lecture delivered at the Institute of Commonwealth Studies, University of London, 27 October.
3. Also, Olowu, D., 'African Governance and Civil Service Reforms', in van de Walle, N., Ball, N. and Ramachandram, V., eds., *Beyond Structural Adjustment: The Institutional Context of African Development*, New York: Palgrave Macmillan, Ch. 4.
4. Before these three phases there was an earlier phase, late 1950s to the 1960s which was devoted to implementation of statist policies, Africanisation and professionalising the system of public administration that has been inherited. The main strategy used is technical assistance.

Chapter 5

1. Most of the material on this section draws from Ayee, J. and Crook, R., 2003, '"Toilet Wars": Urban Sanitation Services and the Politics of Public-Private Partnerships in Ghana', *Institute of Development Studies (IDS) Working Paper* No. 213, pp. 1-34.

2. La Town Development Association. La is a poor traditional quarter of Accra inhabited by the La people.

3. This section draws heavily on Ayee, J.R.A., 2006, 'Accountability for Pro-Poor Local Governance in Africa', in Millett, K., Olowu, D. and Cameron, R., eds, *Local Governance and Poverty Reduction in Africa*, Washington: Joint Africa Institute, Ch. 6, pp. 127-150.

4. This section draws heavily on Ayee, J.R.A., 2005, 'Public Sector Management in Africa', African Development Bank, *Economic Research Working Paper Series*, No. 82, 1-56 pp.

Bibliography

AAPAM, 1989, *Public Enterprises Performance and the Privatization Debate: A Review of the Options for Africa*, New Delhi: Asia Publishing House.

African Peer Review Mechanism, 2005, *Country Review Report and Programme of Action of the Republic of Ghana*, June.

Adamolekun, L. ed., 1999a, *Public Administration in Africa: Main Issues and Selected Country Studies*, Boulder, CO: Westview.

Adamolekun, L., 1999b, 'Governance Context and Reorientation of Government' in Adamolekun, L. ed., 1999, *Public Administration in Africa: Main Issues and Selected Country Studies*, Boulder, CO: Westview, Ch. 1: pp. 3-16.

Adamolekun, L., 1999c, 'Decentralization, Subnational Governments and Intergovernmental Relations', in Adamolekun, L. ed., 1999, *Public Administration in Africa: Main Issues and Selected Country Studies*, Boulder, CO.: Westview, Ch. 4.

Adda, W., 1989, 'Privatization in Ghana', in Ramanadham, V.V., ed., *Privatization in Developing Countries*, London: Routledge.

Adams, A.V and Harnett, T., 1996, *Cost Sharing in the Social Sectors of Sub-Saharan Africa: Impact on the Poor*, World Bank Discussion Paper No. 338, Washington DC: World Bank.

Adu, A.L., 1964, *The Civil Service in New African States*, London: Allen and Unwin.

African Development Bank, 2005, *African Development Report 2005: Public Sector Management in Africa*, Oxford and New York: African Development Bank.

Agbodo, E.A., 1994, 'Problems of Privatization' in *Privatization of State-Owned Enterprises in Ghana*, Accra: Friedrich Ebert Foundation.

Amin, S., 1972, 'Underdevelopment and Dependence in Black Africa: Origins and Contemporary Forms', *Journal of Modern African Studies*, Vol. 4, pp. 503-21.

Appiah, F., 1999, *In the Throes of a Turbulent Environment: The Ghanaian Civil Service in a Changing State*, Legon, School of Administration, University of Ghana: Afram Publications, *Management Monograph Series*, No. 1.

Appiah-Kubi, K., 2001, 'State-Owned Enterprises and Privatisation in Ghana', *Journal of Modern African Studies*, Vol. 39, No. 2, June, pp. 197-229.

Appleby, P.H., 1949, *Policy and Administration*, Alabama: University of Alabama Press.

Argyris, C., 1960, *Understanding Organizational Behaviour*, Homewood, IL: Dorsey Press.

Arrow, K., 1985, 'The Economics of Agency', in Pratt, John and Zeckhauser, R. (eds) *Principal and Agents: The Structure of Business*, Boston: Harvard University Press.

Ayee, J.R.A., 1986, 'Some Thoughts on the Use of the Profitability Criterion in Evaluating State Enterprises in Ghana', *Journal of Management Studies*, 3rd series, Vol. 3, January-December, pp. 142-162.

Ayee, J.R.A., 1989, 'The Ombudsman Experiment in the Kingdom of Swaziland: A Comment', *African Administrative Studies*, CAFRAD, No. 33, pp. 96-106.

Ayee, J.R.A., 1990, 'A Note on the Privatization of State Enterprises in Ghana', *Greenhill Journal of Administration*, Vol. 7, Nos 1 & 2, pp. 10-20.

Ayee, J.R.A., 1991, 'Civil Service Reform under the Provisional National Defence Council', *Journal of Management Studies*, Vol. 7, 3rd series, January-December, pp. 1-12.

Ayee, J.R.A., 1993, 'Complexity of Joint Action: The Implementation of Ministerial Organizations under the PNDC in Ghana', *African Journal of Public Administration and Management*, Vol. II, No. 2, July, pp. 25-43.

Ayee, J.R.A., 1994a, 'Notes on the Commission on Human Rights and Administrative Justice in Ghana under the 1992 Constitution', *Verfassung und Recht in Übersee*, Hamburg, University of Hamburg, Vol. 1, No. 2, pp. 159-170.

Ayee, J.R.A., 1994b, *An Anatomy of Public Policy Implementation: The Case of Decentralization Policies in Ghana*, Aldershot: Avebury.

Ayee, J.R.A., 1994c, 'Corporate Plans and Performance Contracts as Devices for Improving the Performance of State Enterprises', *African Journal of Public Administration and Management*, Vol. III, No. 1, pp. 77-91.

Ayee, J.R.A., 1994d, 'Civil Service Reform in Ghana: An Analysis of the 1993 Civil Service Law', *Journal of Management Studies*, Vol. 11, January-December, pp. 13-25.

Ayee, J.R.A., 1997a, 'Local Government Reform and Bureaucratic Accountability in Ghana', *Regional Development Dialogue*, Vol. 18, No. 2, pp. 86-104.

Ayee, J.R.A., 1997b, 'A Code of Conduct for Public Officials: The Ghanaian Experience', *International Review of Administrative Sciences*, Vol. 63, pp. 369-375.

Ayee, J.R.A., 1998, 'Divestiture Programme in Ghana: Experiences and Lessons', *Ghana Economic Outlook*, Vol. 3, No. 1, pp. 88-98.

Bibliography

Ayee, J.R.A., 1999, 'Ghana' in Ladipo Adamolekun, ed., *Public Administration in Africa: Main Issues and Selected Country Studies*, Boulder, CO.: Westview, Chapter 15.

Ayee, J.R.A., 2001a, 'Civil Service Reform in Ghana: A Case Study of Contemporary Reform Problems in Africa', *African Journal of Political Science*, Vol. 6, No. 1, pp. 1-41.

Ayee, J.R.A., 2001b, *Leadership in Contemporary Africa: An Exploratory Study*, United Nations University Leadership Academy Occasional Papers, *Academic Series*, No. 3, December.

Ayee, J. and Crook, R., 2003, '"Toilet Wars": Urban Sanitation Services and the Politics of Public-Private Partnerships in Ghana', *Institute of Development Studies (IDS) Working Paper* No. 213, pp. 1-34.

Ayee, J.R.A., 2005, 'Public Sector Management in Africa', *African Development Bank Economic Research Working Paper*, Vol. 82, November, pp. 1-56.

Ayee, J.R.A., 2006, 'Accountability for Pro-Poor Local Governance in Africa', in Karin Millett, Dele Olowu and Robert Cameron, eds, 2006, *Local Governance and Poverty Reduction in Africa*, Washington: Joint Africa Institute, Ch. 6, pp. 127-150.

Azarya, V., 1988, 'Reordering State-Society Relations: Incorporation and Disengagement', in Rothchild, D. and Chazan, N., eds, *The Precarious Balance: State and Society in Africa*, Boulder and London: Westview Press.

Badu, Y.A. and Parker, A., 1992, 'The Role of Non-Governmental Organizations in Rural Development: The Case of Voluntary Workshops Association of Ghana', *Research Review*, Vol. 8, Nos 1 & 2, pp. 28-32.

Balogun, J. and Mutahaba, G. eds, 1989, *Economic Restructuring and African Public Administration: Issues, Actions and Future Choices*, West Hartford: Kumarin.

Balogun, J. and Mutahaba, G. eds., 1999, 'Redynamizing the Civil Service for the 21st Century: Prospects for a Non-Bureaucratic Structure', *African Journal of Public Administration and Management*, Vol. XI, No. 2, pp. 1-30.

Barzelay, M., 1992, *Breaking Through Bureaucracy: A New Vision for Managing in Government*, Berkeley: University of California Press.

Batley, R., 1994, 'The Consolidation of Adjustment: Implications for Public Administration', *Public Administration and Development*, Vol. 14, pp. 489-505.

Batley, R., 1996, 'Public and Private Relationships and Performance in Service Provision', *Urban Studies*, Vol. 33, Nos 4 & 5, pp. 723-51.

Batley, R., 1997, *A Research Framework for Analysing Capacity to Undertake the 'New Roles' of Government*, Birmingham: Development Administration Group, The University of Birmingham, Paper 23.

Bayliss, K., 2003, 'Utility Privatization in sub-Saharan Africa: A Case Study of Water', *Journal of Modern African Studies*, Vol. 41, No. 4, pp. 507-531.

Bennell, P., 1997, 'Privatization in Sub-Saharan Africa: Progress and Prospects during the 1990s', *World Development*, Vol. 25, No. 11, pp. 1785-803.

Bennet, S., Russel, S. and Mills, A., 1995, *Institutional and Economic Perspective on Government Capacity to Assume New Roles in the Health Sector: A Review of Experience*,

Birmingham: School of Public Policy, University of Birmingham, *The Role of Government in Adjusting Economies*, Paper 4.

Berg, E., 1993, *Rethinking Technical Assistance*, New York: UNDP.

Bienen, H. and Waterbury, J., 1989, 'The Political Economy of Privatization in Developing Countries', *World Development*, Vol. 17, No. 5, pp. 617-32.

Blackburn, K. and Christensen, J.G., 1989, 'Monetary Policy and Policy Credibility: Theories and Evidence', *Journal of Economic Literature*, Vol. 27, No. 1, pp. 1-45.

Blore, I., 1999, 'Poor People, Poor Services: The Future of Urban Services seen Through Fifty Years' Debate in *Public Administration and Development* and its Predecessors', *Public Administration and Development*, Vol. 19, No. 5, pp. 438-46.

Bjur, W.E. and Caiden, G.E., 1978, 'On Reforming Institutional Bureaucracies', *International Review of Administrative Sciences*, Vol. 4, No. 2, pp. 359-365.

Boudiguel, J-L. and Rouban, F., 1988, 'Civil Service Policies Since 1981: Crisis in Administrative Model or Inertia in Policies?', *International Review of Administrative Sciences*, Vol. 54, No. 2, June, pp. 179-99.

Boston, J., Martin, J., Pallot, J. and Walsh, P., 1996, *Public Management: The New Zealand Model*, Auckland: Oxford University Press.

Braibant, G., 1996, 'Public Administration and Development', *International Review of Administrative Sciences*, Vol. 62, pp. 163-76.

Bratton, M. and Hyden, G. eds, 1992, *Governance and Politics in Africa*, Boulder, CO.: Lynne Rienner.

Bratton, M. and van de Walle, N., 1997, *Democratic Transitions in Africa*, Cambridge: Cambridge University Press.

Bratton, M. and van de Walle, N., 1992, 'Towards Governance in Africa: Popular Demands and State Responses', in Goran Hyden and Michael Bratton, eds, *Governance and Politics in Africa*, Boulder, CO.: Lynne Rienner.

Brautigam, D., 1996, 'State Capacity and Effective Governance' in Ndulu, B. and Van der Walle, N., eds, *Agenda for Africa's Economic Renewal*, Washington DC: Translations Publishers for the Overseas Development Council.

Brautigam, D., 1996, 'State Capacity and Effective Governance' in Ndulu, B. and Van der Walle, N., eds, *Agenda for Africa's Economic Renewal*, Washington DC: Translations Publishers for the Overseas Development Council.

Brown, K., Kiragu, K. and Villadsen, S., 1995, 'Uganda Civil Service Reform Case Study Final Report', London and Copenhagen: Overseas Development Administration and DANIDA.

Bryant, C. and White, L., 1982, *Managing Development in the Third World*, Boulder, CO.: Westview.

Buchanan, J.M., 1986, *Liberty, Market and State*, Brighton: Wheatsheaf.

Buchanan, J.M. et al., 1978, *The Economics of Politics*, London: Institute of Economics Affairs.

Buchanan, J.M., 1987, *The Constitution of Economic Policy*, Stockholm: Nobel Foundation.

Butler, S., 1985, *Privatizing Federal Spending: A Strategy to Eliminate the Budget Deficit*, New York: Universe Books.

Caiden, G. E., 1969, *Administrative Reform*, Chicago: Aldine.

Caiden, G.E., 1973, 'Development, Administrative Capacity and Administrative Reform', *International Review of Administrative Sciences*, Vol. 38, No. 4, pp. 327-44.

Caiden, G. E., 1976, 'Implementation: the Achilles Heel of Administrative Reform', in A. F. Leeman, ed., *The Management of Change*, The Hague: Nijhoff Press.

Caiden, G.E., 1978, 'Administrative Reform: A Prospectus', *International Review of Administrative Sciences*, Vol. XLIV, pp. 106-120.

Caiden, G.E., 1988, 'The Vitality of Administrative Reform', *International Review of Administrative Sciences*, Vol. 54, No. 3, September, pp. 331-57.

Caiden, G.E., 1991, *Administrative Reform Comes of Age*, New York: Walter de Gruyter.

Campbell, B.K. and Loxley, J., eds, 1989, *Structural Adjustment in Africa*, New York: St. Martins.

Campbell, T., Peterson, G. and Brakarz, J., 1991, *Decentralization in Local Government in Latin American Countries: National Strategies in Local Response in Planning, Spending and Management*, Washington DC: World Bank, Latin American and Caribbean Technical Department, *Regional Studies Progress Report*, No. 5.

Caulfield, Janice, 2006, 'The Politics of Bureau Reform in Sub-Saharan Africa', *Public Administration and Development*, Vol. 26, pp. 15-26.

Chazan, N., Mortimer, R., Ravenhill, J., and Rothchild, D., 1992, *Politics and Society in Contemporary Africa*, Boulder, CO.: Lynne Rienner.

Cheema, G.S. and Rondinelli, D.A., eds, 1983, *Decentralization and Development: Policy Implementation in Developing Countries*, Beverly Hills: Sage.

Christensen, J.G., 1988, 'Withdrawal of Government: A Critical Review of an Administrative Problem in its Political Context', *International Review of Administrative Sciences*, Vol. 54, No. 1, March, pp. 37-65.

Clapham, C., 1996, *Africa and the International System: The Politics of State Survival*, Cambridge: Cambridge University Press.

Cohen, B.J., 1973, *The Question of Imperialism: The Political Economy of Dominance and Dependence*, New York: Basic Books.

Cohen, J.M., 1993, 'Importance of Public Service Reform: The Case of Kenya', *Journal of Modern African Studies*, Vol. 31, No. 3, pp. 449-76.

Collin, P. and Kaul, M., 1995, 'The Public Service in the Political Transition: An Overview', *Public Administration and Review*, Vol. 15: 207-9.

Collins, P. ed., 2000, *Applying Public Administration in Development: Guideposts to the Future*, Chichester: Wiley.

Collins, P., 2000, 'State, Market and Civil Society: Towards Partnership?', in Collins, P., ed., *Applying Public Administration in Development: Guideposts to the Future*, Chichester: Wiley.

Commins, S.K. ed., 1988, *Africa's Development Challenges and the World Bank: Hard Questions, Costly Choices*, Boulder, CO.: Lynne Rienner.

Cook, P. and Kirkpatrick, C., eds, 1988, *Privatization in Less Developed Countries*, Brighton: Wheatsheaf.

Conyers, D., 1989, 'The Management and Implementation of Decentralized Administration', in *Decentralized Administration in Africa: Policies and Training Experience*, London: Commonwealth Secretariat.

Conyers, D., 2007, 'Decentralization and Service Delivery: Lessons from Sub-Saharan Africa', *IDS Bulletin*, Vol. 38, No. 1, pp. 18-32.

Corkery, J., O'Nuallain, and Wettenhall, R. eds, 1994, 'Public Enterprise Boards: What they are and what they can do', *Asian Journal of Public Administration*, Hong Kong: Department of Political Sciences, University of Hong Kong.

Cowan, G., 1990, *Privatization in the Developing World*, New York: Praeger.

Craig, J., 2001, 'Putting Privatization into Practice: The Case of Zambia Consolidated Copper Mines Limited', *Journal of Modern African Studies*, Vol. 39, No. 3, September, pp. 389-410.

Crook R.C. and Manor, J., 1998, *Democracy and Decentralisation in South Asia and West Africa: Participation, Accountability and Performance*, Cambridge and New York: Cambridge University Press.

Crook, R.C., 2004, 'The State of the State in Africa: What Is To Be Done?', Inaugural Lecture delivered at Beveridge Hall, Senate House, University of London, 27 October.

Cross, J., 1998, *Informal Politics: Street Vendors and the State in Mexico City*, Stanford: Stanford University Press.

Crozier, M., 1964, *The Bureaucratic Phenomenon*, Chicago: University of Chicago Press.

Currie, L., 1978, 'The Objectives of Development', *World Development*, Vol. 6, No. 1, pp. 1-12.

Davis, T., 1990, *Review and Evaluation of Ghana's Civil Service Reform Programme, 1987-1989*, Ottawa, Canada, World Bank Consultant's Report.

Davis, P., 1986, 'Public-Private Partnerships: Improving Urban Life', *Proceedings of the Academy of Political Science*, Vol. 36, No. 2, pp. 10-21.

de Guzman, R.P. and Reforma, M.A., 1992, 'Administrative Reform in the Asian Pacific Region: Issues and Prospects', in Zhijian, Z., de Guzman, R.P. and Reforma, M.A., eds, *Administrative Reform Towards Promoting Productivity in Bureaucratic Performance*, Manila: EROPA.

de Merode, L., 1991, *Civil Service Pay and Employment Reform in Africa: Selected Implementation Experiences*, New York: The World Bank, Institutional Development and Management Division, Africa Technical Department, *Division Study Paper*, 2.

Demongeot, P., 1994, 'Market-oriented Approaches to Capacity Building in Africa', *Public Administration and Development*, Vol. 14, pp. 479-87.

DeLancey, V., 2001, 'The Economies of Africa', in Gordon, A.A. and Gordon, D.L., eds, *Understanding Contemporary Africa*, 3rd ed., Boulder and London: Lynne Rienner, Ch. 5, pp. 101-42.

Denhardt, R., and Denhardt, J., 2000, 'The New Public Service: Serving Rather than Steering', *Public Administration Review*, Vol. 60, No. 6, pp. 549-59.

Devas, N., Delay, S. and Hubbard, M., 2001, 'Revenue Authorities: Are They the Right Vehicle for Improved Tax Administration', *Public Administration and Development*, Vol. 21, pp. 211-22.

Devas, N. and Korboe, D., 2000, 'City Governance and Poverty: The Case of Kumasi', *Environment and Urbanization*, Vol. 12, No. 1, pp. 123-35.

Devas, N., 2001, *Urban Governance and Poverty: Lessons from Tens Cities in the South*, Birmingham: The School of Public Policy, University of Birmingham.

Dia, M., 1993, *A Governance Approach to Civil Service Reform in Sub-Saharan Africa*, Washington DC: The World Bank, *World Bank Technical Paper* No. 225.

Dia, M., 1996, *Africa's Management in the 1990s and Beyond: Reconciling Indigenous and Transplanted Institutions*, Washington DC: The World Bank.

Dixon, J. Kouzmin, A. and Korac-Kakabadse, N., 1998, 'Managerialism – Something Old, Something Borrowed, Little New: Economic Prescriptions Versus Effective Organizational Change in Public Agencies', *International Journal of Public Sector Management*, Vol. 11, Nos 2 & 3, pp. 164-87.

Dodoo, R., 1996, 'The Core Elements of Civil Service Reform', *African Journal of Public Administration and Management*, Vols 5-7, No. 2, pp. 12-35.

Dodoo, R., 1997, 'Performance Standards and Measuring Performance in Ghana', *Public Administration and Development*, Vol. 17, pp. 115-21.

Dodoo, R., 1998, 'Country Paper Ghana', paper delivered at the Second Biennial Pan-African Conference of Ministers of Civil Service under the theme 'Public Service in Africa: New Challenges, Professionalism and Ethics', held in Rabat, Morocco, 13-15 December.

Doig, A., 1995, 'Good Government and Sustainable Anti-Corruption Strategies: A Role for Independent Anti-Corruption Agencies?', *Public Administration and Development*, Vol. 15, No. 2, May, pp. 151-65.

Dordunoo, C.K., 1997, *Management Development in African Countries with Privatization Programmes: The Cases of Ghana, Tanzania and Uganda*, Geneva: International Labour Organisation.

Dorraj, M., 1994, 'Privatization, Democratization and Development in the Third World: Lessons of a Turbulent Decade', *Journal of Development Studies*, Vol. X, pp. 173-85.

Downs, A., 1967, *Inside Bureaucracy*, Boston: Little, Brown & Co.

Dror, Y., 1976, 'Strategies for Administrative Reform' in Leeman, A. F., ed., *The Management of Change*, The Hague: Nijhoff Press.

Dunleavy, P. and Hood, C., 1994, 'From Old Public Administration to New Public Management', *Public Money and Management*, July/September, pp. 9-16.

Dwivedi, O.P., 1985, 'Ethics and Values of Public Responsibility and Accountability', *International Review of Administrative Sciences*, Vol. LI, No. 1, pp. 61-6.

Dwivedi, O.P. and Nef, J., 1982, 'Crises and Continuities in Development Theory and Administration: First and Third World Perspectives', *Public Administration and Development*, Vol. 2, No. 1, pp. 59-77.

Dwivedi, O.P., 1994, *Development Administration: From Underdevelopment to Sustainable Development*, New York and London: St. Martin's Press.

Easter, C. ed., 1993, *Strategies for Poverty Reduction*, London: Commonwealth Secretariat.

Easterly, W. and Levine, R., 1996, *Africa's Growth Tragedy: Policies and Ethnic Divisions*, Development Discussion Paper No. 536, May.

Economic Commission for Africa (ECA), 2003, *Public Sector Management Reforms in Africa* Addis Ababa: Economic Commission for Africa.

EDI and ISAS, 1992, 'Civil Service Reform: Its Role in the South Pacific', *Report of the Seventh Conference of Heads of Public Service in the South Pacific*, Fiji: Institute of Social and Administrative Studies (ISAS), University of South Pacific.

Edwards, J. and Dearkin, N., 1992, 'Privatism and Partnership in Urban Regeneration', *Public Administration*, Vol. 70, autumn, pp. 359-68.

Eggertson, T., 1990, *Economic Behaviour and Institutions*, Cambridge: Cambridge University Press.

Elbadawi, I.A., 1996, 'Consolidating Macroeconomic Stabilization and Restoring Growth in Africa', in B. Ndulu and van de Walle, N., eds, *Agenda for Africa's Economic Renewal*, New Brunswick and Oxford: Transaction, Ch. 1, pp. 49-80.

Elbadawi, I.A. and Gelb, A., 2003, 'Financing Africa's Development Toward a Business Plan?', in van de Walle, N., Ball, N., and Ramachandram, V., eds, *Beyond Structural Adjustment: The Institutional Context of African Development*, New York: Palgrave Macmillan, Ch. 2, pp. 35-75.

Englebert, P., 2000, *State Legitimacy and Development in Africa*, Boulder, CO.: Lynne Rienner.

Englebert, P., 2000, *State Legitimacy and Development in Africa*, Boulder/London, Lynne Rienner.

Esman, M.J., 1988, 'The Maturing of Development Administration', *Public Administration and Development*, Vol. 8, No. 2, June, pp. 125-34.

Esman, M.J., 1991, *Management Dimensions of Development – Perspectives and Strategies*, West Hartford, CT: Kumarin Press.

Francis, P. and James, R., 2003, 'Balancing Rural Poverty Reduction and Citizen Participation: The Contradictions of Uganda's Decentralization Programme', *World Development*, Vol. 31, No. 2, pp. 325-37.

Fernandes, P., 1986, *Managing Relations Between Government and Public Enterprises*, Geneva: International Labour Organisation.

Flanders, S., 1995, 'More Power to Local Authorities', London: Financial Times, 6 October.

Frederickson, G.H., 1996, 'Comparing the Reinventing Government Movement with the New Public Administration', *Public Administration Review*, Vol. 53, No. 3, pp. 214-29.

Fiszbein, A., 1997, 'The Emergence of Local Capacity: Lessons from Colombia', *World Development*, Vol. 20, No. 7, pp. 1029-43.

Fiszbein, A. and Lowden, P., 1999, *Working Together for a Change: Government, Civic and Business Partnerships for Poverty Reduction in Latin America and the Caribbean*, Washington DC: The World Bank.

Fiszbein, A., 2000, 'Public-Private Partnerships as a Strategy for Local Capacity Building: Some Suggestive Evidence from Latin America', in Collins, P., ed., *Applying Public Administration in Development: Guideposts to the Future*, Chichester: Wiley.

Fjeldstad O-H., 2003, 'Fighting Fiscal Corruption: Lessons from the Tanzania Revenue Authority', *Public Administration and Development*, Vol. 23, pp. 165-75.

Fjelstad, O-H., 2001, 'Taxation, Coercion and Donors: Local Government Tax Enforcement in Tanzania', *Journal of Modern African Studies*, Vol. 39, No. 2, pp. 289-306.

Fosler, R.S. and Berger, R.A., eds, 1982, *Public-Private Partnership in American Cities*, Toronto: Lexington Books.

Frank, A.G., 1971, *The Development of Underdevelopment*, New York: Monthly Review Press.

Frantzen, A., 1998a, *Improvement of the Management of Public Toilet Facilities in Kumasi. Roles of Public and Private Sector*. Amsterdam: Institute of Planning and Demography, University of Amsterdam, *Ghana Research Papers*, No. 9.

Frantzen, A., 1998b, *Public-Private Partnerships as a Solution to the Improvement of Public Toilet Facilities: The Case of Kumasi, Ghana*, Nijmegen: Catholic University of Nijmegen.

Frantzen, A. and Post, J., 2001, 'Public Toilets in Kumasi: Burden or Boon?', in Adarkwa, K.K. and Post, J., eds, *The Fate of the Tree: Planning and Managing the Development of Kumasi, Ghana*, Accra: Woeli Publishing.

Ghai, D., ed., 1991, *The IMF and the South: The Social Impact of Crisis and Adjustment*, London: Zed Books.

Ghana, Republic of, 1992, Civil Service Reform Programme: Evaluation-Aide Memoire, May.

Ghana, Republic of (n.d.), *Civil Service Performance Improvement Programme 'The Way Forward'*, Accra: Office of the Head of the Civil Service.

Glentworth, G., 1973, 'Public Enterprises in Developing Countries: Some Suggestions in Creation, Organization and Control', *Journal of Administration Overseas*, Vol. 12, No. 3, July, pp. 1-12.

Glentworth, G., 1989, 'Strategic Issues in Civil Service Reform', unpublished paper delivered at an ODA Conference 'Civil Service Reform in Sub-Saharan Africa', Regent's College, London, 29-31 March.

Goldsmith, A., 2000, 'Sizing Up the African State', *Journal of Modern African Studies*, Vol. 38, No. 1, pp. 1-20.

Goldsmith, A.A., 2001, 'Risk, Rule and Reason: Leadership in Africa', *Public Administration and Development*, Vol. 21, No. 2, May, pp. 77-87.

Golooba-Mutebi, F., 2004, 'Reassessing Popular Participation in Uganda', *Public Administration and Development*, Vol. 24, pp. 289-304.

Gordon, A.A. and Gordon, D.L. eds, 2001, *Understanding Contemporary Africa* 3rd ed., Boulder, CO: Westview.

Gordon, D.F., 1990, 'The Political Economy of Economic Reform in Kenya', Washington DC: Centre for Strategic and International Studies.

Gordon, D.L., 2001, 'African Politics', in Gordon A.A., and Gordon, D.L., eds, *Understanding Contemporary Africa*, 3rd ed., Boulder and London: Lynne Rienner, Ch. 4, pp. 55-99.

Gough, K., 1999, 'The Changing Nature of Urban Governance in Peri-Urban Accra, Ghana', *Third World Planning Review*, Vol. 21, No. 4, pp. 393-410.

Gough, K.V. and Yankson, P.W.K., 2000, 'Land Markets in African Cities: The Case of Peri-Urban Accra, Ghana', *Urban Studies*, Vol. 37, No. 13, pp. 2485-500.

Goulet, D., 1992, 'Development: Creator and Destroyer of Values', *World Development*, Vol. 20, No. 3, pp. 467-75.

Gow, J.I. and Dufour, C., 2000, 'Is the New Public Management a Paradigm? Does it Matter?', *International Review of Administrative Sciences*, Vol. 66, pp. 573-97.

Grindle, M.S. & Thomas, J.W., 1991, *Public Choices and Policy Change: The Political Economy of Reform in Developing Countries*, Baltimore and London: The Johns Hopkins Press.

Grosh, B. and Mukandala, R.S., eds, 1994, *State-Owned Enterprises in Africa*, Boulder, CO.: Westview Press.

Gyimah-Boadi, E., 1991, 'State Enterprises Divestiture: Recent Ghanaian Experiences', in Rothchild, D., ed., *Ghana: The Political Economy of Recovery*, London: Lynne Rienner.

Halfani, M., 1997, 'The Challenge of Governance in Africa: Institutional Change and Knowledge Gaps' in Swilling, M. ed., *Governing Africa's Cities*, Johannesburg: Witswatersrand University Press.

Haile-Mariam, Y. and Mengistu, B., 1988, 'Public Enterprises and the Privatization Thesis in the Third World', *Third World Quarterly*, Vol. 10, No. 2, pp. 1565-87.

Hanf, K. and Scharpf, F.W., eds, 1979, *Interorganizational Policy Making: Limits to Coordination and Central Control*, London: Sage.

Haque, S., 2001, 'The Diminishing Publicness of Public Service under the Current Mode of Governance', *Public Administration Review*, Vol. 6, No. 1, January/February, pp. 65-82.

Harbeson, J.W., 2001, 'Local Government, Democratization and State Reconstruction in Africa: Towards Integration of Lessons from Contrasting Eras', *Public Administration and Development*, Vol. 21, No. 2, May, pp. 89-99.

Hawranek, P.M., 2000, 'Governance of Economic Development: The Institutional and Policy Framework for Public-Private Partnerships – A normative Approach', *International Journal of Public-Private Partnerships*, Vol. 3. No. 1, September, pp. 15-30.

Heckathorn, D.D. & Maser, S.M., 1987, 'Bargaining and the Sources of Transaction Costs: The Case of Government Regulation', *Journal of Law, Economics and Organization*, Vol. 3, No. 1, pp. 69-98.

Hemming, R. & Mansor, A.M., 1988, *Privatization and Public Enterprises*, Washington DC: IMF, *IMF Occasional Paper*, No. 56.

Herbst. J., 1990, 'The Politics of Privatization in Africa', in Suleiman, E.N. and Waterbury, J., eds., *The Political Economy of Public Sector Reform and Privatization*, Boulder, CO: Westview.

Herbst, J., 2000, *States and Power in Africa*, Princeton: Princeton University Press.

Hicks, N. and Kubisch, A., 1984, 'Cutting Government Expenditures in LDCs', *Finance and Development*, September, pp. 37-44.

Hodgson, G., 1988, *Economics and Institutions*, Cambridge: Polity Press.

Hood, C.,1991, 'A Public Management for all Seasons', *Public Administration*, Vol. 69, No. 1, pp. 3-19.

Hood, C., 1995, 'Contemporary Public Management: A New Global Paradigm', *Public Policy and Administration*, Vol. 10, No. 2, pp. 104-117.

Hope Sr., K.R., 2002, 'From Crisis to Renewal: Towards a Successful Implementation of the New Partnership for Africa's Development', *African Affairs*, Vol. 101, No. 404, July, pp. 387-402.

Hope, K.R., 2000, 'Corruption and Development in Africa' in Hope, K.R. and Chikulo, B.C., eds, *Corruption and Development in Africa: Lessons from Country Case-Studies*, London: Macmillan, Ch. 1, pp. 17-39.

Hyden, G., 1983, *No Shortcuts to Progress: African Development Management in Perspective*, Berkeley and Los Angeles: University of California Press.

Islam, N., 1993, 'Public Enterprise Reform: Managerial Autonomy, Accountability and Performance Contracts', *Public Administration and Development*, Vol. 13, No. 2, pp. 129-52.

Islam, N. and Henault, G.M., 1979, 'From GNP to Basic Needs: A Critical Review of Development and Development Administration', *International Review of Administrative Sciences*, Vol. XLV, No. 3, pp. 253-67.

Jacoby, H., 1976, *The Bureaucratization of the World*, Berkeley: University of California Press.

Jackson, R.H. and Rosberg, C.G., 1982, 'Why Africa's Weak States Persist: The Empirical and the Juridical in Statehood', *World Politics*, Vol. 27, October, pp. 1-24.

Jeffries, R., 1993, 'The State, Structural Adjustment and Good Government in Africa', *Journal of Commonwealth & Comparative Studies*, Vo. 31, No. 1, March, pp. 20-35.

Jenkins, G.P., 1994, 'Modernization of Tax Administration: Revenue Boards and Privatization as Instruments of Change', *Bulletin for International Fiscal Documentation*. Vol. 48, February, pp. 75-81.

Jreisat, J.E., 1988, 'Administrative Reform in Developing Countries: A Comparative Perspective', *Public Administration and Development*, Vol. 8, No. 1, pp. 85-97.

John, P., 2002, *Analyzing Public Policy*, London and New York: Continuum.

Jones, R.A., 2000, 'A Role for Public-Private Partnerships in an Enlarged European Union', *International Journal of Public-Private Partnerships*, Vol. 3, No. 1, September, pp. 31-44.

Joshi, A. and Moore, M.P., 2003, 'Institutionalised Co-production: Unorthodox Public Service Delivery in Challenging Environments', *Journal of Development Studies*, Vol. 13, No. 2, pp. 23-37.

Joshi, A. & Ayee, J., 2002, 'Taxing for the State? Politics, Revenue and the Informal Sector in Ghana', *IDS Bulletin*, Vol. 33, No. 3, July, pp. 90-7.

Kaul, M., 1996, 'Civil Service Reforms: Learning from Commonwealth Experiences', *Public Administration and Development*, Vol. 16, pp. 131-50.

Kerf, M. and Smith, W., 1996, *Privatizing Africa's Infrastructure – Promise and Challenge*, Washington DC: The World Bank, *World Bank, Technical Paper* No. 337, *Africa Region Series*.

Kernaghan, K., 1993, 'Partnership and Public Administration: Conceptual and Practical Considerations', *Canadian Public Administration*, Vol. 36, No. 1, pp. 57-76.

Kettl, D., 1997, 'The Global Revolution in Public Management: Driving Themes, Missing Links', *Journal of Policy Analysis and Management*, Vol. 16, pp. 446-62.

Khan, M., 1981, *Administrative Reform: A Theoretical Perspective*, Dacca: Centre for Administrative Studies.

Kikeri, S., Nellis, J. and Shirley, M., 1992, *Privatization: The Lessons of Experience*, Washington DC: The World Bank.

King, R., Inkoomi, D. and Abrampah, K.M., 2001, 'Urban governance in Kumasi: poverty and exclusion', Birmingham: University of Birmingham: Institute of Development Department, *Urban Governance, Partnership and Poverty Working Paper* No, 23, May.

Kiser, E. and Baker, K., 1994, 'Could privatization increase the efficiency of tax administration in less developed countries?' *Policy Studies Journal*, Vol. 22, No. 3, pp. 489-500.

Korten, D., 1980, 'Community Organization and Rural Development: A Learning Process', *Public Administration Review*, Vol. 40, No. 5, pp. 480-511.

Klitgaard, R., 1997, 'Cleaning up and Invigorating the Civil Service', *Public Administration and Development*, Vol. 17, No. 5, pp. 487-509.

Kumssa, A., 1996, 'The Political Economy of Privatization in Sub-Saharan Africa', *International Review of Administrative Sciences*, Vol. 62, pp. 75-87.

Kolderie, T., 1986, 'The Two Different Concepts of Privatization', *Public Administration Review*, Vol. 46, No. 4, pp. 185-291.

Lalaye, M., 1999, 'Public Enterprises' in Adamolekun, L., ed., *Public Administration in Africa: Main Issues and Selected Country Studies*, Boulder, CO.: Westview, Ch. 3, pp. 28-48.

Lane, J.E., 1993, *The Public Sector: Concepts, Models and Approaches*, London: Sage.

Lane, J.E., 1997, 'Introduction: Public Sector Reform: Only Deregulation, Privatisation and Marketization', in Lane, J.E., ed., *Public Sector Reform: Rationale, Trends and Problems*, London: Sage.

Langseth, P., 1995, 'Civil Service Reform in Uganda: Lessons Learned, *Public Administration and Development*, Vol. 15, pp. 365-90.

Larbi, G.A., 1995, *Implications and Impact of Structural Adjustment on the Civil Service: The Case of Ghana*, Birmingham: University of Birmingham, Development Administration Group, Paper 2.

Larbi, G.A., 1998, 'Implementing New Public Management Reforms in Public Services in Ghana: Institutional Constraints and Capacity Issues', unpublished PhD thesis, Birmingham: University of Birmingham, School of Public Policy.

Larbi, G.A., 1999, *The New Public Management Approach and Crisis States*, Geneva: UN Research Institute for Social Development, *UNRISD Discussion Paper* No. 112.

Larbi, G.A., 1998, 'Institutional Constraints and Capacity Issues in Decentralizing Management in Public Services: The Case of Health in Ghan', *Journal of International Development*, Vol. 10, No. 3, pp. 377-86.

Laryea-Adjei, G., 2000, 'Building Capacity for Urban Management in Ghana: Some Critical Considerations', *Habitat International*, Vol. 24, pp. 391-401.

Leftwich, A., 1993, 'Governance, the State and the Politics of Development', *Development and Change*, Vol. 25, No. 2, pp. 363-86.

Lewis, P. ed., 1998, *Africa: Dilemmas of Development and Change*, Boulder, CO.: Westview.

Leys, C., 1976, 'The 'Overdeveloped' Post-Colonial State: A Reevaluation', *Review of African Political Economy*, No. 5, January-April, pp. 39-48.

Leys, C., 1975, *The Underdevelopment of Kenya*, London: Heinemann.

Levy, B., 2004, 'Governance and Economic Development in Africa: Meeting the Challenge of Capacity Building' in Levy, B. and Sahr, K., eds, *Building State Capacity in Africa: New Approaches, Emerging Lessons*, Washington DC: The World Bank, Ch. 1.

Lienert, I., 1998, 'Civil Service Reform in Africa: Mixed Results after 10 Years', *Finance and Development*, Vol. 35, No. 2, pp.1-7.

Lienert, I. and Modi, J., 1997, *A Decade of Civil Service Reform in Africa*, Washington: IMF, *IMF Working Paper*, WP/97/179.

Lindblom, C.E., 1959, 'The Science of "Muddling" Through', *Public Administration Review*, Vol. 19, pp. 79-88.

Lledo, V., Schneider A. & Moore, M., 2004, 'Governance, Taxes and Tax Reform in Latin America', Brighton: Institute of Development Studies, *IDS Working Paper*, 221.

Luke, F.D., 1990, 'Central Agencies, State Capacity and the Current Wave of Structural Adjustment Reforms in Sub-Saharan Africa', *International Review of Administrative Sciences*, Vol. 56, No. 3, September, pp. 431-46.

Lynn (Jnr.), L., 1987, *Managing Public Policy*, Boston: Little, Brown.

Macgregor, J., Peterson, S. and Schuftan, C., 1998, 'Downsizing the Civil Service in Developing Countries: the Golden Handshake Option Revisited', *Public Administration and Development*, Vol. 18, pp. 61-76.

Madison, J., Hamilton, A. and Jay, J., 1788, *The Federalist Papers*, London: Penguin 1987 edition.

Makara, S., 2000, 'Decentralization for Good Governance and Development: Uganda's Experience', *Regional Development Dialogue*, Vol. 21, No.1, spring, pp. 73-92.

March, J.G. and Olsen, J.P., 1989, *Rediscovering Institutions*, New York: Free Press.

March, J.G. and Olsen, J.P., eds, 1976, *Ambiguity and Choice in Organizations*, Oslo: Universitetsförlaget.

Manning, N., 2001, 'The Legacy of the New Public Management in Developing Countries', *International Review of Administrative Sciences*, Vol. 67, pp. 297-312.

Mawhood, P., 1993, 'Decentralization: The Concept and Practice' in Mawhood, P., ed., *Local Government in the Third World: Experience of Decentralization in Tropical Africa*, 2nd edition, Pretoria: Africa Institute of South Africa.

McCourt, W., 1998, 'Civil Service Reform Equals Retrenchment? The Experience of "Rightsizing and Retrenchment" in Ghana, Uganda and the UK', in Minogue, M. et al., eds, *Beyond the New Public Management*, Cheltenham: Elgar, pp. 172-87.

McCourt, W. and Minogue, M., 2001, *The Internationalization of Public Management: Reinventing the Third World State*, Cheltenham: Edward Edgar.

McPake, B.I., 1996, 'Public Autonomous Hospitals in sub-Saharan Africa: Trends and Issues', *Health Policy*, Vol. 35, pp. 155-77.

Metcalfe, L. and Richards, S., 1990, *Improving Public Management*, 2nd edition, London: Sage.

Migdal, J.S., 1988, *Strong Societies and Weak States: State-Society Relations and State Capabilities in the Third World*, Princeton: Princeton University Press.

Mills, G., 2002, *Poverty to Prosperity: Globalization, Good Governance and African Recovery*, Cape Town: South African Institute of International Affairs.

Minogue, M., Polidano, C. and Hulme, D., 1997, 'Reorganizing the State: Towards more Inclusive Governance', *Insight*, No. 23.

Mintzberg, H., 1983, *Structures in Fives*, Englewood Cliffs, New Jersey: Prentice-Hall.

Moe, R.C., 1987, 'Exploring the Limits of Privatization', *Public Administration Review*, Vol. 47, No. 6, pp. 453-60.

Morgan, G., 1986, *Images in Organization*, Beverly Hills, CA: Sage.

Morgan, G., 1990, *Organizations in Society*, London: Macmillan.

Mukandala, R.S., 1992, 'To be or not to be: Paradoxes of African Bureaucracies in the 1990s', *International Review of Administrative Sciences*, Vol. 58, pp. 555-76.

Mukandala, R.S., ed., 2000, *African Public Administration: A Reader*, Harare: African Association of Political Science.

Mule, H., 2001, 'Challenges to African Governance and Civil Society', *Public Administration and Development*, Vol. 21, No. 2, May, pp. 71-76.

Mutahaba, G., 1989, *Reforming Public Administration for Development: Experiences from Eastern Africa*, West Hartford: Kumarin.

Mutahaba, G., Baguma, R. and Halsfani, M., 1993, *Vitalizing African Public Administration for Recovery and Development*, West Hartford: Kumarin.

Myint, H., 1965, *The Economics of the Developing Countries*, New York: Praeger.

Myrdal, G., 1968, *The Asian Drama: An Enquiry into the Poverty of Nations*, New York: Random House.

Nellis, J., 1986, 'Public Enterprise in Sub-Saharan Africa', Washington DC: World Bank, *World Bank Discussion Paper*, No. 1.

Nellis, J., 1989, 'Contract Plans and Public Enterprise Performance', Washington DC: World Bank, *World Bank Discussion Paper*, No. 48.

Nellis, J. & Kikeri, S., 1989, 'Public Enterprise Reform: Privatization and the World Bank', *World Development*, Vol. 17, No. 5, pp. 659-72.

Nellis, J and Shirley, M., 1991, *Public Enterprise Reform: The Lessons of Experience*, Washington DC: The World Bank.

Nickson, A., 1995, *Local Government in Latin America*, Boulder, CO.: Lynne Rienner.

Nickson, R.A., 1997, 'The Public-Private Mix in Urban Water Supply', *International Review of Administrative Sciences*, Vol. 63, No. 2, pp. 165-86.

Nkrumah, S.A., 1992, 'Aspects of Administrative Reforms in Ghana under the PNDC Government', unpublished inter-faculty lecture, University of Ghana, May.

Novick, D., ed., 1960, *Program Budgeting*, Cambridge, MA: Harvard University Press.

Nti, J., 1978, *Civil Service in Ghana: Its Appraisal and Prospects*, Accra: Ghana Universities Press.

Nti, J., 1991, 'The Impact of Economic Crisis on the Effectiveness of the Public Service Personnel', in Balogun, M.J. and Mutahaba, G., eds, *Economic Restructuring and African Public Administration: Issues, Actions and Future Choices*, West Hartford: Kumarin Press.

Nunberg, B., 1996, 'Rethinking Civil Service Reform: An Agenda for Smart Government', Washington DC: The World Bank, PSPD.

Nzouankeu, J.M., 1994, 'Decentralization and Democracy in Africa', *International Review of Administrative Sciences*, Vol. 60, pp. 213-27.

Olowu, D., Williams, A. and Soremekun, K., eds, 1999, *Governance and Democratisation in West Africa*, Dakar: CODESRIA.

Olowu, D. and Smoke, P. eds, 1992, *Public Administration and Development, Special Issue: Successful African Local Government*, Vol. 12, No. 1, pp. 1-122.

Olowu, D., 1997a, 'Decentralisation for Democratic Governance in Africa in the 1990s and Beyond: Issues and Proposed Strategies', *Politeia*, Vol. 16, No. 3, pp. 64-80.

Olowu, D., 1997b, 'Decentralisation for Democratic Governance in Africa in the 1990s and Beyond: Issues and Proposed Strategies', *Politeia*, Vol. 16, No. 3, pp. 64-80.

Olowu, D., 1999a, 'Accountability and Transparency', in Adamolekun, L., ed., 1999, *Public Administration in Africa: Main Issues and Selected Country Studies*, Boulder, CO.: Westview, Ch. 9, pp. 139-58.

Olowu, D., 1999b, 'Redesigning African Civil Service Reforms', *Journal of Modern African Studies*, Vol. 37, No. 1, pp. 1-23.

Olowu, D., 2003, 'African Governance and Civil Service Reforms', in van de Walle, N., Ball, N. & Ramachandram, V., eds, *Beyond Structural Adjustment: The Institutional Context of African Development*, New York: Palgrave Macmillan, Ch. 4, pp. 101-30.

Olowu D. and Wunsch, J.S., 2004, Local Governance in Africa: the Challenges of Democratic Decentralization, Boulder, CO.: Lynne Rienner.

Olsen, J.P., 1982, *The Rise and Decline of Nations*, New Haven, CT: Yale University Press.

Osborne, D. and Gaebler, T., 1992, *Reinventing Government: How the Entrepreneurial Spirit is Transforming the Public Sector*, Reading: Addison-Wesley.

Ostrom, E., 1996, 'Crossing the Great Divide: Co-production, Synergy and Development', *World Development*, Vol. 24, No. 6: pp. 1073-87.

Ottaway, M. ed., 1997, *Democracy in Africa: The Hard Road Ahead*, Boulder, CO: Lynne Rienner.

Oyediran, O. and Agbaje, A. eds, 1999, *Nigeria: Politics of Transition and Governance, 1986-1996*, Dakar: CODESRIA.

Parsons, T., 1951, *The Social System*, Glencoe, Illinois: The Free Press.

Parsons, T., 1960, *Structure and Process in Modern Societies*, New York: The Free Press.

Paul, S., 1992, 'Accountability in Public Service: Exit, Voice and Control', *World Development*, Vol. 20, No. 7, pp. 1047-61.

Perrow, C., 1986, *Complex Organizations: A Critical Theory*, 3rd edition, New York: Random House.

Peters, B.G., 1992, 'Government Reorganization: A Theoretical Analysis', *International Political Science Review*, Vol. 13, No. 2, June, pp. 199-217.

Peterson, S.B., 1998, 'Saints, Demons, Wizards and Systems: Why Information Technology Reforms Fail or Under-perform in Public Bureaucracies in Africa', *Public Administration and Development*, Vol. 18, pp. 37-60.

Peterson, G.E., 1997, *Decentralization in Latin America: Learning Through Experience*. Washington DC: World Bank, *Viewpoints. Latin American and Caribbean Studies Series*.

Pierre. J., ed., 1998, *Partnerships in Urban Governance: European and American Experience*, London: Macmillan.

Pollitt, C., 1993, *Managerialism and the Public Services: The Anglo-American Experience*, 2nd edition, Oxford: Blackwell.

Post, J., 1999, 'The Problems and Potentials of Privatizing Solid Waste Management in Kumasi, Ghana', *Habitat International*, Vol. 23, No. 2, pp. 201-15.

Powell, V., 1987, *Improving Public Enterprise Performance*, Geneva: International Labour Organisation.

Pozen, R., 1976, *Legal Choices for State Enterprises in the Third World*, New York: New York University Press.

Pressman, J. L. and Wildavsky, A., 1984, *Implementation*, Berkeley: University of California Press.

Prud'homme, R., 1995, 'The Dangers of Decentralization', *The World Bank Research Observer*, Vol. 10, No. 2, August, 201-20.

Public Administration and Development, 1998, *Special Issue, Symposium on Government Ownership and Enterprise Management*, Vol. 18, No. 3.

Quah, J.S.T., 1976, 'Administrative Reform: A Conceptual Analysis', *Philippine Journal of Public Administration*, Vol. 20, No. 1, pp. 50-67.

Ramanadham, V.V., 1984, *The Nature of Public Enterprise*, London: Croom Helm.

Ramanadham, V.V., ed., 1989, *Privatization in Developing Countries*, London: Routledge.

Ramanadham, V.V., ed., 1995, *Privatization and Equity*, London: Routledge.

Rasheed, S., Beyene, A. and Otobo, E., eds, 1994, *Public Enterprise Performance in Africa: Lessons from Country Case Studies*, Ljubljana: International Centre for Public Enterprises and United Nations Economic Commission for Africa (UNECA).

Rasheed, S, and Olowu, D. eds, 1993, *Ethics and Accountability in African Public Services*, Nairobi: UNECA.

Riggs, F., 1964, *Administration in Developing Countries: The Theory of Prismatic Society*, Boston: Houghton Mufflin.

Riggs, F. eds, 1970, *Frontiers of Development Administration*, Durham: Duke University Press.

Rizos, E.J., 1965, 'Country Development: The New Ethic of Public Administration', *International Review of Administrative Sciences*.vol 31, No 4, pp 279-288.

Robinson, M., 2007, 'Does Decentralization Improve Equity and Efficiency in Public Service Delivery Provision?', *IDS Bulletin*, Vol. 38, No. 1, January, pp. 7-17.

Rondinelli, D.A. and Iacono, M., 1996, 'Strategic Management of Privatization: A Framework for Planning and Implementation', *Public Administration and Development*, Vol.16, pp. 247-63.

Rondinelli, D.A. et al., 1989, 'Analysing Decentralization Policies in Developing Countries: A Political Economy Framework', *Development and Change*, Vol. 20, pp. 57-87.

Rostow, W.W., 1959, 'The Stages of Economic Growth', *The Economic History Review*, August.

Rothchild, D. and Chazan, N., eds, 1988, *The Precarious Balance: State and Society in Africa*, Boulder and London: Westview.

Rowat, D.C., ed., 1980, *International Handbook on Local Government Reorganization: Contemporary Developments*, London: Aldwych Press.

Rweyamamu, A.H. and Hyden, G., eds, 1975, *A Decade of Public Administration in Africa*, Nairobi: East African Literature Bureau.

Samonte, A.G., 1970, 'Patterns and Trends in Administrative Reform', in Lee, H-B. and Samonte, A.G., eds, *Administrative Reforms in Asia*, Manila: EROPA, pp. 287-302.

Sandbrook, R., 1985, *The Politics of Africa's Economic Stagnation*, Cambridge: Cambridge University Press.

Sandbrook, R., 1993, *The Politics of Africa's Economic Recovery*, Cambridge: Cambridge University Press.

Savas, E.S., 1985, *Privatizing the Public Sector: How to Shrink Government*, London: Chatham House.

Savas, E.S., 1987, *Privatization: The Key to Better Government*, London: Chatham House.

Savas, E.S.,1989, *A Typology of Market-Type Mechanisms*, Paris: OECD, *PUMA Market-Type Mechanisms Series*.

Schaffer, B.B., 1969, 'The Deadlock in Development Administration', in Leys, C., ed., *Politics and Change in Developing Countries*, Cambridge: Cambridge University Press.

Schivo-Campo, S., 1998, 'Government Employment and Pay: The Global and Regional Evidence', *Public Administration and Development*, Vol. 18, pp. 457-78.

Sen, A., 1999, *Development as Freedom*, Oxford: Oxford University Press.

Shirley, M.M., 1983, *Managing State Owned Enterprises*, Washington DC: The World Bank, *World Bank Staff Working Paper*, No. 577.

Shirley, M., 1989, *The Reform of State Owned Enterprises: Lessons from World Bank Lending*, Washington DC: The World Bank, *PPR Series*, No. 4 .

Shivji, I., 1991, 'The Democracy Debate in Africa: Tanzania', *Review of African Political Economy*, Vol. 50, March, pp. 79-91.

Silvani, C. and Baer, K., 1997, *Designing a Tax Administration Reform Strategy: Experiences and Guidelines*, Washington DC: IMF.

Simon, H.A., 1947, *Administrative Behaviour*, New York: Macmillan.

Sinclair, M.D., 1999, 'Regulation and Facilitation of Public-Private Partnerships: The MSP Policy Framework', *Development Southern Africa*, Special Issue, Vol. 16, No. 4, summer.

Sindane, J., 2000, 'Public-Private Partnerships: Examining Solid Waste Management in Khayelitsha-Cape Town, South Africa', *International Journal of Public-Private Partnerships*, Vol. 3, No. 1, September, pp. 103-32.

Skocpol, T., 1985, 'Bringing the State Back In: Strategies of Analysis and Current Research', in Evans, P., Rueschemeyer, D. and Skocpol, T., eds, *Bring the State Back In*, Cambridge: Cambridge University Press.

Smith, B.C., 1985, *Decentralisation: The Territorial Dimension of the State*, London: Allen and Unwin.

Smith, L., 2003, 'The Power of Politics: The Performance of the South African Revenue Service and some of its Implications', *Policy: Issues and Actors*, Johannesburg: Centre for Policy Studies, Vol. 16, No. 2, April, pp. 1-19.

Spiering, W.D., 2000, 'Public-Private Partnership in City Revitalization – A Dutch Example', *International Journal of Public-Private Partnerships*, Vol. 3, No. 1, September, pp. 133-44.

Squires, G., ed., 1989, *Unequal Partnerships: The Political Economy of Urban Redevelopment in Postwar America*, New Brunswick: Rutgers University Press.

Stapenhurst, F. and Langseth, P., 1997, 'The Role of the Public Administration in Fighting Corruption', *International Journal of Public Sector Management*, Vol. 10, No. 5, pp. 311-30.

Stella, P., 1993, 'Tax Farming: A Radical Solution for Developing Country Tax Problems?', *IMF Staff Papers*, Vol. 40, No. 1, pp. 217-25.

Stephenson, M.O., 1991, 'Whither the Public-Private Partnerships: A Critical Overview', *Urban Affairs Quarterly*, Vol. 27, No. 1, pp. 109-27.

Stiglitz, J.E., 1987, 'Principal and Agent' in Eatwell, J., Milgate, M. & Nennan, P., eds, *The New Palgrave Dictionary of Economics*, London: Macmillan.

Stone, D.C., 1965, 'Government Machinery Necessary for Development', in M. Kriesberg, ed., *Public Administration in Developing Countries*, Washington DC: The Brookings Institution.

Stowe, K., 1992, 'Good Piano won't Play Bad Music: Administrative Reform and Good Governance', *Public Administration*, Vol. 70, No. 3, autumn, pp. 35-45.

Strehl, F., 1993, 'Implementation of a New Performance Appraisal System and the Problems of Organizational Change', *International Review of Administrative Sciences*, Vol. 59, pp. 83-97.

Suleiman, E.N. and Waterbury, J., eds, 1990, *The Political Economy of Public Sector Reform and Privatization*, Boulder, CO: Westview.

Sullivan, H.J., 1987, 'Privatization of Public Services: A Growing Threat to Constitutional Rights', *Public Administration Review*, Vol. 47, No. 6, pp. 461-7.

Swerdlow, I., 1975, *The Public Administration of Economic Development*, New York: Praeger.

Talierco, R., 2003, *Designing Performance: The Semi-Autonomous Revenue Authority Model in Africa and Latin America*, Washington DC: The World Bank.

Talierco, R., 2004, 'Administrative Reform as Credible Commitment: The Impact of Revenue Autonomy on Revenue Authority Performance in Latin America', *World Development*, Vol. 32, No. 2, pp. 213-32.

Tangri, R., 1999, *The Politics of Patronage in Africa*, Oxford: James Currey.

Tangri, R., 1991, 'The Politics of State Divestiture in Ghana', *African Affairs*, Vol. 90, No. 361, pp. 523-36.

Tanzi, V. and Zee, H., 2001, *Tax Policy for Developing Countries*, Washington DC: IMF. *IMF Economic Issues* series.

Temu, A.E. and Due, J.M., 2000, 'The Business Environment in Tanzania after Social-ism: Challenges of Reforming Banks, Parastatals, Taxation and the Civil Service', *Journal of Modern African Studies*, Vol. 38, No. 4, pp. 683-712.

Tendler, J., 2001, 'Small Firms, the Informal Sector and the Devil's Deal', *IDS Bulletin*, Vol. 33, No. 3, July, pp. 98-104.

Tennyson, R., ed., 1994, *Tools for Partnership Building*, London: The Prince of Wales Business Leaders' Forum, *Partnership Handbook Series*, No. 2.

Therkildsen, O., 1993, '"Successful African Local Government": Some Methodological and Conceptual Issues', *Public Administration and Development*, Vol. 13, pp. 501-5.

Therkildsen, O., 2001, Efficiency, Accountability and Implementation: Public Sector Reform in East and Southern Africa, Geneva: UNRISD, *Programme Paper*, No. 3.

Therkildsen, O., 2001, 'Understanding Taxation in Poor African Countries: A Critical Review of Selected Perspectives', *Forum for Development Studies*, Vol. 1, June, pp. 99-123.

Thioub, I., Diop, M-C. and Boone, C., 1998, 'Economic Liberalization in Senegal: Shifting Politics of Indigenous Business Interests', *African Studies Review*, Vol. 41, No. 2, September, pp. 63-89.

Thomas, P.G. (1996) 'Beyond the Buzzwords: Coping with Change in the Public Sector', *International Review of Administrative Sciences*, Vol. 62: 5-29.

Thompson, K.E.E., 1999, *Capacity Building for Community Management. Integrated Development for Water Supply and Sanitation*, Addis Ababa: Water Engineering Development Centre Conference.

Thornhill, W., 1985, *Public Administration*, Cambridge: ICSA Publications.

Tivey, L. ed., 1981, *The Nation-State: The Formation of Modern Politics*, Oxford: Oxford University Press.

Todaro, M., 2000, *Economic Development*, 7th edition, Reading, MA: Addison-Wesley.

Tordoff, W. ed., 1985, *Government and Politics in Africa*, Bloomington: Indiana University Press.

Tordoff, W., 1994, 'Decentralisation: Comparative Experience in Commonwealth Africa', *The Journal of Modern African Studies*, Vol. 32, No. 4, December, pp. 555-80.

Toye, J. and Moore, M.P., 1998, 'Taxation, Corruption and Reform', in Robinson, M., ed., *Corruption and Development*, London and Portland, Oregon: Frank Cass.

Tullock, G., 1970, *Private Wants, Public Means*, New York: Basic Books.

Turner, M. and Hulme, D., 1997, *Governance, Administration and Development: Making the State Work*, New York: Palgrave.

Udogu, E.I. ed., 1997, *Democracy and Democratization in Africa: Toward the 21st Century*, Leiden: Brill.

United Nations (UN), 1961, *A Handbook of Public Administration: Current Concepts and Practice with Special Reference to Developing Countries*, New York: UN.

UN, 1975, *Development Administration: Current Approaches and Trends in Public Administration for National Development*, New York: UN.

Bibliography

UNDP, 1995, *Public Sector Management, Governance and Sustainable Human Development*, New York: UNDP.

UNDP, 1997, *Governance for Sustainable Growth and Equity*, New York: UNDP.

UNDP, 2001, *World Public Sector Report: Globalization and the State, 2001*, New York: UNDP.

Van de Walle, N., 1994, 'The Politics of Public Enterprise Reform in Cameroon', in Grosh, B and Mukandala, R., eds, *State-Owned Enterprises in Africa*, Boulder, CO.: Westview Press.

Van de Walle, N., 2001, 'The Economic Correlates of State Failure', in Robert Rotberg, ed., *When States Fail*, Princeton: Princeton University Press.

Van de Walle, N., 2003, 'Introduction: The State and African Development', in van de Walle, N., Ball, N., and Ramachandram, V., eds, *Beyond Structural Adjustment: The Institutional Context of African Development*, New York: Palgrave Macmillan.

Vuylsteke, C., 1988, 'Techniques of Privatization of State-Owned Enterprise', Washington DC: World Bank, *World Bank Technical Paper*, 88, Vol. 1.

Waddington, C.J. and Enyimayew, D.A., 1989, 'A Price to Pay: The Impact of User Charges in Ashanti-Akim District, Ghana', *International Journal of Health Planning and Management*, Vol. 4, pp. 17-47.

Waddington, C.J. and Enyimayew, D.A., 1990, 'A Price to Pay, Part 2: The Impact of User Charges in the Volta Region of Ghana', *International Journal of Health Planning and Management*, Vol. 5, pp. 287-312.

Walsh, K., 1995, *Public Services and Market Mechanisms: Competition, Contracting and the New Public Management*, London: Macmillan.

Webster, A., 1984, *Introduction to the Sociology of Development*, London: Macmillan.

Weaver, R.K. and Rockman, B.A., 1993, *Do Institutions Matter?*, Washington DC: Brookings Institution.

Weber, M., 1978, *Economy and Society*, Vols I-II, Berkeley: University of California Press.

Weimer, D.L. and Vining, A.R., 1996, 'Economics' in Kettl, D. F. and Milward, H. B., eds, *The State of Public Management*, Baltimore and London: The Johns Hopkins University Press.

Werlin, H. (1992) 'Linking Decentralization and Centralization: A Critique of the New Development Administration', *Public Administration and Development*, Vol. 12 (October): 201-15.

Westott, C., 1999, 'Guiding Principles on Civil Service Reform in Africa: an Empirical Review', *The International Journal of Public Sector Management*, Vol. 12, No. 2, pp. 145-70.

Whittington, D., Lauria, D.T., Choe, K., et al., 1993, 'Household Sanitation in Kumasi, Ghana: A Description of Current Practices, Attitudes, and Perceptions', *World Development*, Vol. 21, No. 5, pp. 733-48.

173

Wildavsky, A., 1979, *Speaking Truth to Power: The Art and Craft of Policy Analysis*, Boston: Little, Brown & Co.

Wildavsky, A., 1984, *The Politics of the Budgetary Process*, Boston: Little, Brown & Co.

Wildavsky, A., 1985, 'The Logic of Public Sector Growth', in Lane, J-E., ed., *State and Market: The Politics of the Public and the Private*, London: Sage.

Wiley, J., 2001, 'African Governance and Civil Society: Equity, Efficiency and Participation', *Public Administration and Development, Special Issue* Vol. 21, No. 2, May, pp. 71-186.

Williams, W. and Elmore, R.F., eds., 1976, *Social Programme Implementation*, New York: Academic Press.

Williamson, O., 1986, *Economic Organization*, London: Harvester Wheatsheaf.

Wilson, W., 1887, 'The Study of Administration', *Political Science Quarterly*, Vol. 2, pp. 197-222.

Wohlmuth, K., 1997/98, 'Good Governance and Economic Development in Africa: An Introduction', in Wohlmuth, K., Bass, H.H., and Messner, F., eds, *Good Governance and Economic Development, African Development Perspective Yearbook, 1997/98*, Hamburg: LIT VERSAG.

World Bank, 1981, *Accelerated Development in Sub-Saharan Africa*, Washington DC: The World Bank.

World Bank, 1989, *Sub-Saharan Africa: From Crisis to Sustainable Growth*, Washington DC: The World Bank.

World Bank, 1994, *World Development Report 1994: Infrastructure for Development*, New York: Oxford University Press.

World Bank, 1995, *A Continent in Transition: Sub-Saharan African in Mid-1990s*, Washington DC: The World Bank.

World Bank, 1995a, *World Development Report 1995*, New York: Oxford University Press.

World Bank, 1995b, *Bureaucrats in Business: The Economics and Politics of Government Ownership*, Oxford: Oxford University Press.

World Bank, 1996a, *Public Enterprise and Privatization in Ghana*, Washington DC: World Bank, Technical Assistance Project.

World Bank, 1996b, *World Development Report 1996: From Plan to Market*, New York: Oxford University Press.

World Bank, 1997a, *World Development Report 1997: The State in a Changing World*, Washington DC: The World Bank.

World Bank, 1997b, *The World Bank Annual Report 1997*, Washington DC: The World Bank.

World Bank, 1999, *The World Bank Annual Report 1999*, Washington DC: The World Bank.

World Bank, 2000a, *Entering the 21st Century, World Development Report,* New York: Oxford University Press.

World Bank, 2000b, *Can Africa Claim the 21st Century,* Washington DC: The World Bank.

World Bank, 2002, *Building Institutions for Markets World Development Report 2002,* New York: World Bank.

World Bank, 2003, *Sustainable Development in a Dynamic World: Transforming Institutions, Growth, and Quality of Life, World Development Report, 2003,* New York: Oxford University Press.

World Bank, 2004, *Making Services Work for Poor People, World Development Report 2004,* New York: Oxford University Press.

Wunsch, J.S. and Olowu, D. eds, 1995, *The Failure of the Centralized State: Institutions and Self-Governance in Africa,* San Francisco: ICS Press.

Wunsch, J.S., 1995a, 'Foundations of Centralization: The Colonial Experience and the African Context' in Wunsch, J.S. and Olowu, D., eds, 1995a, *The Failure of the Centralized State: Institutions and Self-Governance in Africa,* San Francisco: ICS Press, Ch. 2.

Wunsch J.S., 1995b, 'Centralization and Development in Post-Independence Africa' in Wunsch, J.S. and Olowu, D. eds. (1995a) *The Failure of the Centralized State: Institutions and Self-Governance in Africa* (San Francisco: ICS Press), Ch. 3.

Wunsch, J., 2000, 'Refounding the African State and Local Governance', *The Journal of Modern African Studies,* Vol. 38, No. 3, September, pp. 487-509.

Wunsch, J., 2001, 'Decentralization, Local Governance and 'Recentralization' in Africa', *Public Administration and Development,* Vol. 21, No. 4, October, pp. 277-88.

Wunsch, J.S. and Ottemoeller, D., 2004, 'Uganda: Multiple Levels of Local Governance', in Olowu, D. and Wunsch, J.S., *Local Governance in Africa: The Challenges of Democratic Decentralization,* Boulder, Co.: Westview.

Yankson, P.W.K., 2000, 'Community-Based Organizations (CBOs) and Urban Management and Governance in an Era of Change in Ghana: The Case of the Greater Accra Metropolitan Area', *Ghana Social Science Journal,* new series, Vol. 1, No. 1, January, pp. 97-139.

Young, R.A., 1991, 'Privatization in Africa', *Review of African Political Economy,* Vol. 51, July, pp. 50-62.

Young, C., 1988, 'The African Colonial State and Its Political Legacy', in Rothchild, D. and Chazan, N., eds, *The Precarious Balance: State and Society in Africa,* Boulder, CO.: Westview, pp. 25-66.